My Rachel

S.J. Gibbs

J.M. McKenzie

DEDICATION

For Rachel.

Yours is a story that deserves to be told.

.

ACKNOWLEDGEMENTS

S.J. Gibbs is Rachel's mother. She started writing Rachel's story many years ago but found it too difficult due to her emotional involvement.

J.M. McKenzie is a friend and fellow writer, who offered to take up the mantle after S.J. reached out for help.

Both authors want to acknowledge the support of their fellow writers and members of JAMS Publishing: AJ Jones, who did the proofreading and editing; and Michael Andrews, who did the formatting for publication.

They also want to acknowledge the patience and encouragement of their partners, Steve and Mike, and all their family and friends.

Table of Contents

Prologue

I sat in the back of the ambulance, bracing myself as it raced through the deserted city streets. I held Rachel's hand, trying to reassure her and keep her as comfortable as possible on the narrow trolley, supporting her limbs with pillows to prevent them from being bruised as they knocked against the metal side rails.

It wasn't the first time we had been in the back of an ambulance together being rushed to hospital, and it wouldn't be the last. But this time was different. This time it was in the middle of a global pandemic: a pandemic that had already claimed thousands of lives and would go on to claim many more.

The usual flashbacks and feelings of panic and anxiety were worse than ever. They threatened to overwhelm me, but I fought them away. I had to keep calm, remain in control. Rachel needed me. She was in pain. She was in danger. She was being admitted to a hospital that was full of people with

Covid-19. I had to look after her.

I had spent the last 33 years protecting her, fighting for her, representing her, talking to her: 33 years fighting for my beautiful daughter's life; 33 years fighting for her rights; 33 years on a never-ending roller coaster of sorrow, and of joy.

Today was going to be no different. I was terrified, but I knew I could do it. I had to. For Rachel.

For her, I am strong. I am resilient. I have to be. I can never give up fighting for her. If I don't do it, who will?

I am Shelley. I am Rachel's mother. I am her voice. Rachel will never be able to tell her story, but I will tell it for her.

Chapter One – The Beginning

I'll begin at the beginning, because that is where it all began.

Rachel was born on Wednesday, the 20th of May, 1987, at 8am.

Until that day, my life had been pretty normal. I wasn't academic and left school at 15 to go into business, as was our family tradition. My dad was a successful business man and at that time owned a welding supply company. He supported and encouraged me to follow in his footsteps, and I opened my own first business when I was just 16. I went into partnership with my boyfriend at the time, buying and selling second-hand and rare records from a small shop in Birmingham.

I met Giles, Rachel's father, when I was 17. I went

on a date with one of his friends to an engagement party, but he caught my eye as soon as I arrived. The rest is history, as they say.

From that day, we started seeing each other, and he proposed when I was 20. It didn't seem right to carry on in business with my ex-boyfriend, so I sold the record business and started working with my dad in his sales division. Giles was a few years older than me and worked as a skilled toolmaker in the motor industry. Together we managed to save the deposit to buy a house, and I had my first mortgage at 20.

Giles moved into the house straight away, but my parents wouldn't let me join him until after we were married. As a small concession, I was allowed to stay there on Saturday nights.

We were married three days after my 21st birthday in August, 1985. Life was good. We were in love; we had a lovely home and good jobs. Everything was perfect. We waited a year before planning to start a family and I was pregnant by the following September.

Soon after I became pregnant, I moved into an office-based administrative role. Life as a sales representative could be tiring and demanding. I wanted to take good care of myself and my baby. We were so excited. Everyone was. The baby was to be the first grandchild for both sets of parents.

The day before Rachel was born, I had spent the day with my parents. My due date was the 15th of June, a few weeks away, and I was enjoying my maternity leave. My pregnancy had been pretty easy. Everything had been completely normal throughout. I felt great and Baby was doing well. It was the start of what would turn out to be a lovely summer. We enjoyed a leisurely lunch on the patio, looking out over the garden. Dad was a keen gardener and the long, well-kept lawn, and neat colourful beds, stretched down to a park that ran across the bottom of the property. We sipped our ice-cold drinks and chatted excitedly about the impending addition to our family. Would it be a boy or a girl? What would he or she look like? What colour hair and eyes would it have? Would it look most like me or Giles?

We had decorated the nursery in neutral colours, but secretly I was hoping for a little girl. I remember thinking, though, that none of it really mattered as long as the baby was healthy.

Towards the end of the day, I became aware that the baby hadn't been moving as much as usual. I mentioned it to Mum, but we reassured each other that, as the end of the pregnancy approached, it could be normal to notice reduced movement, as there is less space for the baby to move around. She told me to put my feet up for a while and offered to cook dinner for Giles when he got home from work.

By the time we had finished dinner, I couldn't remember feeling any movement at all since I had first mentioned it to Mum in the afternoon. I told Giles I was concerned and was grateful when he didn't try to reassure me but insisted that we go straight to the hospital to get everything checked out. He knew I hated being a bother and would never have mentioned it if I wasn't genuinely worried.

Nevertheless, when we arrived at the local Maternity Unit at around 6pm, I felt like a complete fraud. It was chaos. The staff were rushed off their feet. Everyone else in the crowded waiting room seemed to be in agony. I gave up my seat for one woman who, if the intensity of her screaming was anything to go by, must have been going to give birth imminently. I was worried that I was making a fuss about nothing. I tried to melt quietly into the background as woman after woman went through before us, all seemingly so much more worthy than me of receiving urgent attention. Giles was not so patient. He was becoming increasingly agitated.

"Can't you moan and scream a little bit?" he semi-joked. "We're never going to get seen at this rate!"

Eventually, we were taken through to a tiny cubicle. The examination couch almost filled the entire space. Giles stood awkwardly at the end of the couch, trying to keep out of the way as the midwife examined me. I was struggling with my emotions, flitting between guilt that I was wasting their valuable time, and concern that I had still not felt my baby move. Apart from that, I felt absolutely fine.

I explained to the midwife why I was there, and she wired me up to a monitor. Within a few minutes, she was reassuring us that everything was fine. She said we'd done the right thing and that it was always important to get checked out in these circumstances. She suggested that we stay on the monitor for a half hour or so and, if everything remained fine, we could go home. I remember feeling slightly jealous of the moaning and screaming women outside in the waiting room. They were going to meet their babies soon, but I was going to have to wait a while longer.

Even though the midwife was adamant that everything was fine, I still wasn't entirely convinced. It was hard to do anything else but watch the rolling paper that flowed from the machine. A line at the bottom tracked any contractions, and nothing much was going on there. Another line at the top, tracked my baby's heart rate. From time to time, the heart rate seemed to be slowing down, and at times nothing at all was being recorded. The midwife blamed it all on the machine. She fussed about with the pads on my tummy.

"These machines are more trouble than they're

worth. Don't worry. Everything's fine. The transducers can't get a good connection. It must be baby's position."

I hoped she was right. I looked at Giles. He was frowning. I wanted to cry. I already felt so much love for this tiny being inside of me. This little person that I was responsible for, that it was my duty to protect. I had to trust the midwife. She knew what she was doing. What did I know? I just had a feeling. That was all. Just a feeling. I told myself not to be silly.

A short time later, we were on our way home. The midwife had given me a "kick chart" to record my baby's movements on. She'd told me that, starting from the next day, if I hadn't felt ten kicks by the time I went to bed, I should come back to the hospital. In the meantime, we were to attend our next routine antenatal appointment the following week.

I'd felt another pang of envy as the cries of another woman in labour echoed down the corridor as we made our way back to the car. How long would I have to wait until that was me? How long until I could welcome my baby into the world?

As it turned out, I wasn't going to have to wait as long as I thought. By 11pm, we were back, and this time I was in labour. Or at least that's what I thought. Since about 8pm, I'd been having contractions, and at 10pm, when they were regular and coming every 5 minutes, we decided to head back to the hospital.

It seemed busier than ever. But I didn't have to wait and was taken straight through to an assessment room. We saw a different midwife. She was curt and offhand, and I was made to feel as if I was wasting their time. Ironically though, this time I felt that I did need to be there. To me, the contractions felt strong and painful, but the midwife told me that they were most likely Braxton Hicks contractions, which were simply an indication that my uterus was practising for the real thing.

I was examined internally and put back on a monitor again. She told me that my cervix was still closed, and I was definitely not in labour yet. I was devastated. I was in real pain. I couldn't believe that this wasn't labour. If it wasn't, I doubted that I'd be able to cope with the real thing. I could barely cope now.

I was surprised and upset when she gave me a couple of sleeping pills and told me that I was going to be transferred up to the ward where they could keep an eye on me. It was a postnatal ward, for women who had already had their babies, as they had no room on the labour ward or the antenatal ward, for women who were still pregnant. Giles was told that he would have to go home and come back in the morning, as they couldn't have visitors on the ward at night, when new mothers were trying to sleep.

I began to feel an ominous sense of foreboding after Giles left, and I was taken up to a quiet and eerie four-bedded bay on the ward. The other three beds were occupied by new mothers and their babies, who were tucked up cosily in plastic cots beside their beds. They were all sleeping peacefully.

No-one seemed to be listening to me. They didn't seem to believe what I was saying about my contractions. Another brusque nurse, whom I assumed to be another midwife, bossed me into bed and strapped me up to another monitor. After telling me again in no uncertain terms that I wasn't in labour yet, she pulled the curtains around me, handed me the buzzer, and told me to call if I needed anyone.

And that was that. I was left alone in the dark, surrounded by sleeping women, clutching the buzzer, and watching the paper flow from the machine for the third time that day. Again, even in the semi-darkness I could see my baby's heart rate slowing down every few minutes, but this time I could see spikes on the bottom of the tracing each time I had a contraction. A tear rolled down my cheek. A short time later, the nurse came back and took me off the monitor. She told me everything was fine, and I should try to get some rest. She then handed me the buzzer again and disappeared.

I couldn't settle. I was still in pain. I waited as long as I could before pressing the buzzer again.

"It hurts. Please help me," I begged when she reappeared.

"My dear, you're disturbing everybody on the ward! There are three new mothers in here who need their rest. Try to get some sleep. You'll need your strength tomorrow."

"Could I have something for the pain? Maybe some gas and air?" I remembered being told that this was a good pain reliever in early labour.

"We're very busy and we have no gas and air available. Besides, you're not in labour yet. If I were you, I'd save it until you really need it. The sleeping tablets will work soon. Now lie down and try to go to sleep."

I tried to relax like I'd been taught in my antenatal classes, but I was so tense with fear and distress it was impossible. I began to cry in earnest, stifling my sobs with my hand to prevent myself from disturbing anyone. But some of the other women were stirring. One of them looked over at me in annoyance. Anxious not to be seen as a nuisance, I took off my watch and put it on the locker where I could see it. I fixed my gaze on it and tried to wait at least 15 minutes before pressing the buzzer again.

The next few hours were awful. My contractions were getting stronger and longer. I was in agony. I pressed the buzzer every 15 minutes, and the nurse would come back in and tell me to go to sleep. She was becoming more and more irritated. I was in a nightmare of pain. The sleeping pills had no effect. I was wide awake and couldn't get into a comfortable position. I didn't care who I disturbed anymore. I didn't care who I annoyed. I pressed the buzzer again and again. At around 3am, when she reappeared and I'd braced myself for another "telling off", a look of concern finally spread over her face. She told me that she was going to find a midwife to come and look at me, and then she scurried off.

A midwife? Wasn't she a midwife? What was going on? All this time I had thought she was the midwife, and it turned out she wasn't. She was actually an auxiliary.

After what felt like an eternity, she returned with a real midwife who gave me another internal examination.

"Well dear, I'm happy to tell you that you are in labour and you're doing really well. You're already four to five centimeters dilated."

For a moment I felt ecstatic. Thank God! They would get me down to the labour ward now and give me something for the pain. Giles could come back and be with me. Soon, our baby would be here, and this would all be over. But my relief was short lived.

"As you know, we're very busy tonight, and there are no beds free on the labour ward at the moment. We'll try and get you down as soon as we can, but you'll have to hang on for now. In the meantime, we'll pop you on the monitor again to keep an eye on things."

"Can you call my husband? Can he come back now, to be with me?"

"He can't come in until you're on the labour ward, I'm afraid. I'll call him as soon as a bed is available. Leave it with me …"

She hooked me up to the monitor for the fourth time, and then they were gone.

I thought back to my antenatal classes, and everything they had said about what it would be like. Giles would be by my side. We could choose to have whatever pain relief we wanted on the day, depending on how I was coping. It would be painful, but it would also be as calm and relaxed as possible and hopefully a joyous and beautiful experience. I remember thinking I would have been better off giving birth in a field, for all the help they had given me. At least there, I could have screamed my head off without disturbing anyone.

I can't remember how long it was before they came back to take me downstairs. I think it was around 4am. I was lost in a world of pain. I could scarcely breathe. I screamed out again and again, as I was wheeled down seemingly endless corridors, begging for someone to help me, to give me something for the pain. This couldn't be right. Something must be wrong. I was going to die. My baby was going to die. I was terrified.

The room on the labour ward was small and windowless. It was hot and stuffy. I needed air. I was sobbing and gasping for breath as I was transferred onto the bed. Perspiration was dripping down my face. My nightdress was soaked with sweat. I could feel hysteria growing and building inside me, like a volcano threatening to explode.

"Could I have some gas and air now, please?" I managed to get out between contractions.

"I'm sorry! We're really busy. I don't think there's any available, but I'll have another look," someone replied.

"Please ... " I begged.

"Look! I've got to go. Here's the buzzer. I'll be back in a minute."

"Have you called my husband?"

"I have. A few times. But he hasn't answered. We'll try again in a minute."

I screamed after her as she left the room. "I need help! I need someone! Get my husband! Please get my husband!"

More time passed in a fog of pain. Then Giles was at my side. I clutched at his hand. Overjoyed to see him, but angry that he'd not come sooner.

"Where have you been? I needed you."

"I came as soon as they called me." He was confused.

"They said they'd called several times, and you never picked up."

"No, I don't think so."

The midwife bustled back into the room with another monitor. I was becoming familiar with the process now. She set it all up and left the room again.

"It's been awful, Giles. I've been on my own. I've been in agony. No-one cares. Something's wrong, I know it. Please do something. I can't cope anymore. I really can't cope."

"I'm here now. It's going to be ok. I'm sorry. Don't worry."

But I was watching the tracing coming from the machine again. Again, the baby's heart rate seemed to be slowing down, even stopping for short periods. Surely *this* machine wasn't faulty as well?

"Look at the monitor, Giles. It's not working

properly again. Look at the heart rate."

"So much for technology," he grumbled. "They said this afternoon that they're more trouble than they're worth. It's probably faulty, as you say, but I'm going to get them to check it."

He pressed the buzzer. After a while, the midwife reappeared. She fussed with the monitor.

"Is everything alright?" Giles asked.

"Yes, it's just the machine. They play up sometimes. Nothing to worry about."

I was distraught. I was sure something was wrong, but just couldn't seem to get through to anyone. Maybe it was me? Maybe I was just being pathetic. Maybe there were other women in more pain than me, who needed more attention than me and my baby.

I don't know how I got through the rest of that night. It helped that Giles was with me, but I still hadn't had any pain relief. And I was worried. Really worried. We called the midwife back in at least four or five times over the next couple of hours, and every time she said the same thing. "Nothing to worry about. Just the machine ..."

We didn't know what to do. We argued about it. I cried about it. We tried to reassure each other. It was the worst night of our lives.

On the last occasion we called for the midwife, Giles insisted, "How can you be sure? Look at it!"

He pointed to the tracing. "We're not medical, but we can clearly see that the baby's heart rate keeps dropping."

"I'm not concerned. Please don't worry. It's the machine." And she was gone again.

It was 7am before she returned. This time, I thought she did seem a little concerned when she looked at the tracing, but she turned to me with a smile and patted my thigh.

"Right! I finish at 8. Let's try and get this baby out before then, shall we?"

She explained that she was going to try and speed things along by breaking my waters. It was uncomfortable, but I was so relieved that the end was finally in sight, I didn't care.

I felt the warm wetness gushing from me and the pressure inside me altered slightly. She murmured something, partly to herself and partly to us.

I looked at Giles.

"Sorry! What did you say?" Giles asked.

"I said, 'There's some meconium in the waters.'! But don't worry. It happens sometimes, and baby will be out soon."

She left the room. I had no idea what was going on. What was "meconium"? What did it mean if it was in the waters? I could feel hysteria building inside me again. I wanted to scream.

"What does it mean? What does she mean?" I yelled at Giles. "Where's she gone now?"

Then she hurried back in. She darted about the room with an urgency I hadn't sensed before.

"I really can't cope. Please help me," I pleaded with her.

Finally, she gave me an injection.

"Pethidine," she said. "To ease the pain."

It was 7.30am.

Almost as soon as she had given me the painkiller, she seemed to be asking me to push.

Her tone was strident … urgent. "Push! Push! Push! Come on now!"

I pushed. I knew instinctively my baby's life depended on it. I feared that my own life might depend on it. I pushed with everything I had.

A man slipped into the back of the room. He had a stethoscope draped around his neck. A doctor.

He was watching. Waiting. Who was he? What was he doing? What was he waiting for?

At 8am, I finally pushed my baby girl into the world. In a blur of pain and fear, I felt her slither from me.

The room was silent. The midwife hurriedly bundled her up and gave her to the doctor, who was now at the bottom of the bed. Everything happened very quickly after that. I don't even remember the cord being cut. He took my baby to the back of the room and started working on her.

She was pale and floppy. I was numb. I thought she was dead.

Chapter Two – Special Care

Time seemed to stand still as we watched and waited. Giles was standing completely motionless, staring towards the back of the room. The midwife had a hand on my stomach, but her head was turned towards the scene unfolding behind her. I was straining to see past her... straining to hear my baby's first cry. It never came.

"Oh my God," I said aloud to the room. "What's wrong with my baby?"

The doctor was tense and frowning as he sucked dirty brown mucous from her nose and mouth with a long tube, and rhythmically pressed her tiny chest with his fingers. It felt like a lifetime – later, I was told it was only 45 seconds - before she gasped, and he seemed to relax a little. He nodded to the midwife, who turned her attention back to me.

A few moments later, they bundled her up in a blanket and placed her in my arms. Her eyes were closed, and she looked peaceful and calm. She still hadn't cried, but her colour was better and she was breathing. I felt her little heart beating close to mine, watched her tiny chest moving rapidly up and down, heard her little huffs and snuffles. She was alive.

I thought I had plenty of time to enjoy her, but the doctor was hovering close by. I could tell by his manner that he was anxious to whisk her away again. He was saying something about taking her to Special Care ... just for observation.

I tried to take in every detail of her.

"Nothing to worry about," he said.

Her nose, her eyes.

"Just for 24 hours."

Her mouth, her hair.

"You'll be able to see her later."

She was perfect.

Then she was gone.

The midwife finished what she had to do. I was exhausted and in a haze from the painkiller, but my mind was racing. I remember the placenta being delivered, and being told it was intact and healthy, but all I could think about was my baby. Why had the doctor seemed in such a rush to take her away if there was nothing to worry about?

I had torn during the delivery and another doctor

came in and stitched me up. I searched his face, looking for clues, but his expression was blank as he focused on the task at hand. The room was silent. Where was my baby? What were they doing to her? Was she alright?

When they had finished, I asked if I could go and see her.

"Dad can see her for a bit, dear. Then he can go home and let you get some rest. You need to rest now. We're going to take you back upstairs, and you can see her later," the midwife said, her face carefully concealing her emotions.

I didn't want to rest. I wanted to see my baby, but I was too tired to argue. I trusted them. They said she was fine, and I believed them. But my stomach was in knots.

I was taken back up to the same bed, in the same ward where I had spent the night. Everyone was up and about now. Curtains were open, and lights were on. Babies were fussing and crying. Mothers were feeding and changing them. They looked at me and the space beside my bed where my new baby should be tucked up in her plastic cot under her little, pink blanket. Their eyes gave away their shock and curiosity, reinforcing the fact that my baby was missing.

It was impossible to rest. The other mothers kept asking me questions. Where was my baby? What had happened? I couldn't believe how insensitive they were. I tried to close my eyes. I was tired, but I just couldn't sleep. I felt like I was in a bad dream. A dream that, it seemed, was never going to end. Around lunchtime, I was moved into a side room. It was a relief to be on my own, away from prying eyes and awkward questions, but by now the drugs had worn off, and I was wide awake. I was frantic. I asked again and again if I could go and see my baby, but every time I got the same answer. I needed my rest. I'd be able to see her later.

I reflected on this for a moment. All the newborn clothes and nappies I had chosen for my baby lay neatly folded in my bag. I unfolded them and laid them on the bed. A little hat and cotton mittens, a cream baby grow and a soft cardigan. The next time a nurse came in I asked her, "Won't my baby need her clothes?"

"That's not necessary, dear. They have their own clothes in Special Care. They don't wear much actually. Helps the staff to care for them more easily." Her eyes were averted towards the floor.

I folded the clothes and put them back in my bag. I pictured my baby lying in an incubator with nothing on but a nappy. I didn't want her to be naked, nor to be dressed in hospital clothes. I wanted her to wear the clothes that I had chosen for her. I squinted at my watch; time was passing so slowly.

Giles came back in the afternoon with our parents, and it was about 4pm when we were finally taken down to Special Care. I was desperate to see her and was confused and annoyed when, instead of being taken straight to the unit, Giles and I were led into a small meeting room to speak to the doctor first. Our parents all waited anxiously outside in the corridor.

A small, elderly woman bustled into the room. She introduced herself as a paediatrician and explained that she was looking after our baby. Her facial expression was grave. She seemed to choose her words carefully as tears filled my eyes and spilled down my cheeks.

"I'm afraid your baby is very poorly. She's been having fits throughout the course of the day. We've started her on a drug called phenobarbitone to try and control these. She's not managing to breathe for herself, so she's been connected to a ventilator which is doing her breathing for her."

I didn't understand. I felt as though her words had physically struck me. My mind and body reeled with their impact. "All day," she'd said. This had been going on *all day* ... while I was resting upstairs, and Giles was at home celebrating with our parents. He'd gone home believing she was fine. They'd said there was nothing to be concerned about, that it was just for observation, just a precaution. I couldn't make any sense of what she was saying. Stupefied, I just stared at her.

Fits? Breathing difficulties?

I began clutching at straws.

"Could it be asthma? My dad has asthma. I had fits as a baby. It was to do with a fever. Maybe, she has a fever?" I cradled my throbbing head in my arms.

The doctor tapped her forefinger on her temple. "It's more to do with here than it is here." She pointed to her chest. I felt as if I was collapsing from the inside out. Her head? What did she mean? My usually ordered brain was suddenly totally disordered. The happiness I'd felt throughout my pregnancy now shattered. None of this made any sense.

I stood up. "Can we see her now?"

"Yes, of course ... for a few minutes. Come with me."

She took us to the entrance of the unit. There were four clear incubators in the small room, each containing a tiny baby surrounded by an array of machines and infusion pumps. Lights flashed, machines beeped, and ventilators hissed. Nurses with surgical gowns over their uniforms fussed around the babies, turning knobs, and pushing buttons and recording everything they did on clipboards. It was terrifying. One of the nurses was talking to us, giving us more information about what was going on, but my mind neglected to absorb any of it.

Our parents were told they couldn't come into the unit and were guided towards a big glass partition, which they could look through instead. A nurse helped Giles and me put on thin blue gowns that covered our clothes, and papery blue hats like shower caps that covered our hair. I followed her instructions like a robot. My mind was spinning. It didn't feel real. My fingers trembled as I struggled to pull elasticated, blue, plastic bags over my shoes. Yesterday, we'd been sitting on the patio in the sunshine, full of happiness, looking forward to our new arrival, and today we were about to pay our first visit to our baby, who couldn't breathe for herself and had something wrong with her head.

I peered into the incubator. Beneath a jumble of wires and tubes, my baby was sleeping. She was being fed through a tube in her nose. The nurse opened a small window at the side of the incubator and encouraged me to reach in and touch her. I slowly stretched my fingers out towards her, then quickly drew them back. I was afraid - afraid to touch my own baby. What if I dislodged one of the tubes or disconnected a wire? I examined her again for any flaws or imperfections, but there were none.

"It's ok," the nurse reassured me. "You can't hurt her. Go on. Touch her. She needs you." A feeling of helplessness overcame me. I could do no good for my baby, nor for me.

I reached out again, and this time my fingers found their way to hers. She looked so perfect, so beautiful. How could she be so poorly?

I spoke to her. "It's me. Your mother. I'm here now. It's going to be alright. Stay with me. Stay with us," I said.

Whatever the issue was, we could overcome this, couldn't we?

Giles was weeping beside me. I saw our parents watching us from the other side of the glass, their faces masks of pain and anguish. I caught my mother's eye, then looked away. She looked crushed. I couldn't meet her gaze.

When we entered my room back up on the ward, the curtains were billowing and flapping wildly. The sky outside was black with foreboding. Giles and our parents hurried over to close the windows that had been opened earlier to provide some relief from the stifling heat of the past few days. A storm was coming, and it was going to be a big one by the looks of things.

I stood in the doorway and looked at them.

"Even God is angry," I said.

The storm broke. The wind howled, and rain lashed against the windows. Lightening flashed, and thunder rumbled. We watched the banks of rolling clouds constantly shifting and changing shape and colour, and we waited. Waited for some news that she was improving. Waited to be told that we could go back down and see her again. Trying to make some sense of what was happening. Trying to be positive ... to be hopeful. Trying to trust that she was in good hands.

I opened the bible in the drawer beside my bed. It fell open on 2 Chronicles verses 22 to 24. Something about the reign of Ahaziah, a young king of Judah, and his mother, Athaliah. I scanned the pages looking for a sign or some words of comfort but found none. It meant nothing to me.

After an hour or so, the doctor we had met downstairs opened the door.

"Can I speak with the parents on their own, please?"

She ushered our parents from the room and stood at the end of the bed. Giles was standing, and I was sitting on the edge. She looked at us both, seemingly trying to find the right words to say what she had to say. My legs began to tremble.

"I'm sorry to have to tell you this, but I'm afraid your baby is no better. In fact, her condition has deteriorated, and she is now critically ill. It is unlikely that she will survive the night. I'm very sorry."

The room began to spin, and the acrid taste of bile rose in my throat. I thought I was going to be sick. Giles made a strange sound. Not a splutter and not a sob, but something in between.

"If you are religious and would like to have her christened, now might be the right time to do it."

I grabbed at the chance to do something … something that might make a difference. I felt as though everything was totally out of our control. Our daughter's life - our lives - were completely in the control of this small, elderly woman. At last, here was something I could do. I believed in God, and it seemed as if only He could help us now.

It was all arranged very quickly, and a short time later, we were standing around our baby's incubator: a still weeping Giles, a nurse, the hospital chaplain, and me. In a brief, but emotional, ceremony we named our baby, Rachel Fallon. I handed her into God's care. I trusted Him to get her through this. I wasn't going to let her go. He wasn't going to let her go.

When the service was over, I thanked the chaplain and asked him, "When she comes home, will you do another blessing service for her please? One that our friends and family can come to."

He nodded, "Of course!" But his eyes said something else.

The nurse put her hand on my shoulder. "Can you say goodbye to Rachel now? We need to make her comfortable. We'll call you if anything changes."

We allowed ourselves to be led back up to the ward. It

was late, but they said Giles could stay with me. We sat in the small room, barely able to look at each other … unable to comfort each other, our own pain was so raw. Every noise from outside, every footstep, every voice could be the one … the someone who would come through the door to tell us that our baby had died.

But no-one came. All night, we sat like that. Unable to sleep, unable to talk, unable to cry. I swung between grief and rage. Grief for our precious little girl and the life that was going to be snatched away from her before it had even begun. Grief for our own hopes and dreams … dreams that had been so bright and strong only a day before, but which had now dissolved in a pool of tears and pain. Rage about why this had happened to her … to us. Rage about the unfairness of it all. She didn't deserve this. Neither did we!

As the hours passed and no-one came, the grief subsided and the rage took over.

I wasn't a victim - never had been, never would be - and my baby wasn't going to be one either. I wasn't weak and passive. I had taken control of my life aged just 16. I had always known what I wanted and how to get it. Rachel was my daughter, and she was going to be like me. I knew it. She hadn't given up, and neither would I.

What was I doing sitting here, passively waiting for someone to come and tell me that my baby had died? What was I thinking, letting these doctors and nurses tell me what to do and when to do it? Allowing them to decide when I could see her and when I could not! It was time to take back control. Time to fight for my daughter's life.

I straightened my back. Giles was slumped in the chair beside me. I looked at my watch - 5am. I stood up and left the room.

The corridor was dark, but I could see the dim, orange glow at the nurse's station. I walked up to it.

The nurse looked up from whatever she was reading. "Yes, can I help you?"

"Yes, I'd like you to ring Special Care and find out how my baby is. Rachel, Fallon Taylor."

"Well ... "

"No, I'd like you to ring now, please. Yesterday, they told us she may not survive the night. It's 5am. She clearly has, and I want to know how she is."

She looked at me for a moment, then, clearly accepting that she wasn't going to win, picked up the phone.

She asked after Rachel then nodded and listened for a few minutes, doodling on a pad on the desk in front of her. She replaced the receiver and looked up at me.

"She's still critical but stable. No real change."

I was ecstatic. She hadn't given up. She was still fighting. Now she wasn't going to fight on her own. I was going to be there at her side. I was her mother. My place was with her, not sitting in a dark room waiting for her to die. From now on, we were going to do this together!

Chapter Three – Fighting for Life

Straight after breakfast, we were escorted back down to see Rachel. This time, instead of allowing ourselves to be hurried away after our allotted time, I made it clear that we were staying. We were not going back to the ward to sit passively, worrying and praying. Our place was by our baby's side. She needed us and we were going to be there for her.

After a short briefing about the importance of being aware of the other sick babies in the room, respecting the privacy of their parents, and the expectation that we would not disturb the staff and leave the room without hesitation in the case of an emergency, it was agreed that we could stay.

We sat at her side all day. She was still on the ventilator so we couldn't hold her or cuddle her, but I was able to touch her through the holes on the side of the incubator. She slept all the time. I had never seen her open her eyes. The nurse explained it was because of the medication she was on. It was a strong sedative.

I stroked her and talked to her continually. I told her how much she was loved and about all the people who were waiting to meet her. I told her about the nursery we had prepared for her at home, about the beautiful cot waiting for her and the teddy-bear wallpaper. I urged her to be strong and hang on. I told her that we were here for her and always would be.

We did our best to comply with all the instructions we had been given. We left the room when asked. We didn't talk to any of the doctors unless they approached us. We were quiet and considerate, respecting the needs of the other babies and their parents. Nevertheless, it was clear that the staff didn't want us there ... that we were an inconvenience. They were quiet and matter of fact in all their dealings with us.

It was around 6pm when one of the nurses came and sat down to talk to us. Rachel seemed to be doing well, and I thought she was going to tell us that her condition was improving. But her face was serious. My heart sank.

"We're thinking of moving Rachel to another hospital. I just wanted to let you know."

"Moving her! Why?" I was horrified. I looked at her tiny body surrounded by all the tubes and monitors that were keeping her alive.

"It's just that there is another baby unit across town. They might be able to offer her things there that we can't do here?"

"I don't understand. What can they do there that you can't do here? I don't want her to be moved. Wouldn't it be … dangerous?"

"Well, it obviously has some risks, but in the long run …"

"No! I don't want her to be moved. I want her to stay here. She's safe here."

"Well, it's not definite. Don't worry. I just wanted to let you know we were thinking about it." She smiled and patted my arm as she stood up and hurried away.

I looked at Giles in disbelief. He shook his head.

"No way," I said. "No way, is she moving to another hospital on the other side of the city."

Later that evening, we went back up to the ward for some supper and to spend some time with our parents during visiting time. We hadn't been there long when Rachel's paediatrician bustled into the room. She asked to speak to us alone again and went on to explain that Rachel had pulled out her breathing tube and, as she seemed to be breathing fairly well by herself, they had decided not to reconnect her to the ventilator. She stressed that it did not mean she was out of the woods yet, only that they were going to see how she got on.

I was surprised and concerned. They had told me that she was totally dependent on the ventilator to breathe. No-one had suggested that she might be able to breathe on her own. In addition, she was asleep all the time. She had shown no signs of trying to touch the breathing tube all day, let alone pull it out. The tube was firmly attached to her face with sticky tape and the nurses were continually checking that it was in place, and that the ventilator was working properly.

Not totally convinced that the story rang true, I tried to persuade myself that it was a good thing. The first sign of some improvement, but I was uneasy.

"Can I come down and see her please?" I asked. "Maybe I can hold her now?"

"It's late, dear. That's not a good idea. Wait till morning. Let's see how she does."

"But ..."

She cut me off. "It's not appropriate to have parents on the unit at night. There are not enough staff to deal with that. You can come down first thing tomorrow if she remains well."

And so, it was. The prospect of another night, sitting in that room, waiting and worrying. I didn't think I could bear it.

Giles was exhausted and couldn't face another night in a chair. He clearly wasn't coping with the whole situation. I suggested he went home for some rest, and he gratefully agreed.

I tried to lie down and get some sleep myself after he had gone but, despite my own exhaustion, it wouldn't come. I tossed and turned for an hour or so, my mind buzzing with unanswered questions. What was wrong with Rachel? Would she recover? Would she really be able to breathe on her own? How did she manage to pull her tube out? Why had this happened to us? Would she make it through another night? If she did, what would the coming days and weeks bring for us all?

Eventually, I gave up and went to make myself a cup of coffee in the kitchen. There was another woman in there. She was still pregnant but was having some complications. Like me a couple of nights ago, she was waiting for her baby to be born … waiting for her labour to start. I told her our story. It was good to talk to someone not directly involved. She was a good listener.

I told her everything, but when I got to the part about them wanting to move Rachel to another hospital and her pulling her tube out, her face clouded over.

"What's wrong?" I asked.

"Oh, it's probably nothing but … no, I shouldn't say."

My heart was pounding in my chest. "What? Please tell me. What is it? I've got a bad feeling about this. If you know something, you have to tell me."

"Well ..." she began reluctantly. "well, my husband is an engineer here. He was called down to Special Care late this afternoon, because one of the ventilators wasn't working properly." She hesitated.

"Right ... " A knot was forming in the pit of my stomach. "Carry on ... please."

"So, he couldn't fix it, and when he left, the doctors were discussing which baby should be transferred to a hospital across town where another ventilator was available. He was shocked that they were having to make decisions like that."

I couldn't speak. I didn't want to even consider what her words might mean.

They wouldn't do that. They couldn't.

Chapter Four – Small Improvements

Rachel did get through that night without needing to be put back on the ventilator. She got through the next one, and the one after that. She was a fighter, our daughter.

For the next few days, I spent every waking hour at her side. As her condition slowly improved, she spent more and more time out of the incubator. Now, I was able to hold her, and cuddle her, and kiss her. As they gradually reduced her medication, she was awake for longer and longer periods. She began to open her eyes … her beautiful blue eyes. How I loved to stare into those eyes. What was she feeling? What was she thinking? I whispered my thoughts to her, constantly telling her how much she was loved. I had to convince her that life was worth fighting for.

I was able to wash her, change her nappy and

dress her in her own clothes. She began to feel more like my child - my baby. She belonged to me. When she had been lying in the incubator attached to all the tubes and wires, dressed only in a nappy, it had almost felt as though she wasn't really mine, that she was the property of the hospital and the nurses and doctors, and that I was just an interloper - an inconvenience.

No-one ever discussed her feeding with me. At first, she was fed through a tube in her nose. They never asked me if I wanted to breast feed her, so I just assumed it was not an option. Neither did they ever ask me if I wanted to express my own milk for her. I just never thought to ask. There were too many other things to think and worry about, and Giles and I were both tired beyond anything we'd experienced before. It was a deep exhaustion brought about, not only from lack of sleep, but from the strain of the emotions constantly running through us. But, whenever Rachel opened her eyes it was as though a radiant sun suddenly shone in my life, and all feelings of tiredness instantly faded away.

After a couple of days, the nurses started giving her small amounts of milk from a bottle, and, when they were happy, they removed the tube and allowed me to feed her, too. It was a difficult job. She didn't seem able to suck and swallow properly. Most of the milk dribbled down her chin. But it was a start, and it helped me to feel even closer to her. To feel like her mother and not a helpless onlooker.

My love for her grew and blossomed every moment I spent with her. She was so special, so incredible, her skin so soft to touch and stroke. Against all the odds, she was growing stronger every day.

As well as our parents, other family and friends started to come and visit, but they were still only able to look at her through the glass. My teenage brother, Den, my best friend, Louise, and a friend of my mother, who had lost her own baby shortly after birth, all came to visit. The love and support we got from them all really helped us through those difficult days. We were not alone. So many people were thinking of us, praying for us, and genuinely wishing us well. Cards and letters began to arrive. I was truly touched by all the messages of love and concern. I read them all to Rachel, telling her how many people were waiting to meet her, begging her to hurry up and get better so she could meet them all.

I learned a lot about myself in those days ... some good things, and some bad. I had to do a lot of growing up very quickly - to face responsibility, to be less selfish, and to learn patience. Plus, it was around this time that material wealth became irrelevant to me. Everything that had mattered so much to me before, suddenly seemed unimportant and insignificant.

But she did seem to be getting better. Every day I

saw small improvements. She was awake for longer, her breathing seemed easier, her feeding better. The doctors and nurses spent less time monitoring her and seemed happier. After a week, she was moved out of the small intensive care area and into the nursery, which was -still part of Special Care, but it was an area where the babies were not quite so critical and needed less attention.

She was now in a plastic, see-through cot, like all the other babies had been up on the ward. She was not attached to any machines or wires or tubes, but lay on an "apnoea" blanket, which would send out an alarm if she "forgot to breathe" for a moment. As far as I was concerned, Rachel had been a very poorly baby who was now on the road to recovery. My soul felt brighter, and a smile had returned to my face.

I was barely aware of what treatments and investigations she was having during this time. I knew she had been on phenobarbitone for the fits, but that this medication had been reduced. I also knew that she was on strong antibiotics to kill off any bacteria that had entered her lungs when she inhaled the meconium (the dark, sticky contents of an unborn baby's bowels) during the birth. At the time, I didn't take much notice of these aspects of her care. Nobody ever explained what they were doing and why, or even asked my permission as far as I can recall. I was 22, and had just given birth to my first baby in the most traumatic circumstances imaginable. I was in shock. As far as I was concerned, she was getting better and that was all that mattered. A miracle had occurred, and one I was extremely grateful for.

Four days after the birth, I was discharged. I no longer had a room at the hospital and could only visit Rachel at certain times during the day.

The first day I had to go home without her, I was distraught. I wept for the entire journey and for hours later. I couldn't bear it. I felt as though I was deserting her … being torn apart from her. Once again, she was in the hands of the hospital staff. Once again, they were in control, not me. But now I knew that I was still her mother.

That first night back at home without her was one of the most difficult of my life. I stood in the empty nursery, exactly as it was when I had left it. I had never imagined coming home without my baby. The previous day, my milk had come in. My breasts were hard and swollen. Like my heart, they ached for my baby. I had never expected to be back in that room on my own, the cot cold and empty, the teddy-bear quilt smooth and uncreased. I buried my face in the quilt and sobbed. My throat and chest spasmed in pain. It felt as though my broken heart was trying to escape from my body.

The next couple of weeks were the hardest so far. An exhausting blur of travelling back and forth to the hospital. I was adamant that I wanted them to call me every morning as soon as Rachel woke for a feed. So, I would be up at dawn every morning, showered and dressed, ready to rush over there the moment they called. I tried to give her all her feeds during the day until 10pm and, to be fair, generally the staff supported me in this.

Looking back, I don't know how I did it. Rachel consumed my thoughts day and night. When I wasn't with her, I was just waiting until it was time to go back. When I was asleep, I dreamt that I was with her. We were constantly on edge. Every time the phone rang, we leapt up, fearful that she might have taken a turn for the worse.

Although I was back and forth several times during the day, I actually had less time with her than before. The six-bedded nursery area was busy and cramped, and when we were there, we were constantly being asked to leave and wait outside while the staff attended to another baby.

My life was on pause. I barely slept or ate. Giles went back to work and I didn't really see anyone else. Visitors had dried up as people didn't know where we were going to be and when. Everyone just seemed to be getting on with their lives again. Everyone, that was, except me. Our home was in disarray, neither of us having the energy, nor the motivation to do anything about it. Summer was coming, but the warm summer sunshine did nothing to brighten my spirits.

But Rachel continued to improve, and, after a couple of weeks, the day finally came when they decided that she was well enough to come home. To ensure that we would be able to cope on our own, they arranged for me to spend 48 hours alone with her in a room near Special Care. Those 48 hours were the most precious we had ever spent together. Giles visited in the evenings, but essentially, we had two days alone with each other, just my baby and me. No nurses or doctors interfering. No-one telling me what to do and how to do it, when to go and when to stay.

I was ecstatic. I hardly put her down. I kissed her and danced with her. I sang to her. I laughed and I cried with her. At last, I was her mother, and she was my daughter, already my most perfect friend in the entire world.

Two days later Giles came to the hospital and, together with Rachel, our precious baby daughter, we all went home.

<u>Chapter Five – Home at last</u>

The day we took Rachel home from the hospital, they arranged for her to have a brain scan before we left. They said it was routine for all babies who had been in Special Care. Nothing to worry about. They were concerned about the fits, and that she might have epilepsy, so they had booked her in for another EEG at the main hospital in the city. She was to see her paediatrician for a follow-up appointment in four weeks' time.

As far as we were aware, as we strapped her into her brand-new car seat for the first time, we were taking home a perfectly healthy baby, who may or may not have mild epilepsy.

I sat in the back of the car with her for that first drive home. Her little head kept lolling to one side. I had to support it with my hand. I wasn't impressed with the car seat. Why didn't it come with proper support for the baby's head? It was well known that you had to support a new baby's head carefully until they developed their muscle control. I kissed her. She was tiny. Beautiful. All mine. I was never going to let her out of my sight ever again.

She started to cry almost as soon as we got home. I carried her around the house. Showed her the garden, her nursery, all her toys and the gifts that people had sent for her. She was here. She was alive. She had done it. She was home where she belonged, with the people who loved her ... who would love her and care for her for the rest of her life. If only I had known then what that would come to mean.

Her crying persisted. Nothing seemed to settle her. It wasn't a cry like those of the other babies I had heard in the hospital. It was developing into a high pitched, continuous scream. I began to feel anxious ... panicky, even. Although it was early, maybe she was hungry. In the hospital when she had needed a feed, the nurses just handed me a ready prepared bottle. I shouted to Giles.

"A feed, Giles! She needs a feed!"

I hurried to the kitchen with her still screaming in my arms.

Giles had started to prepare a bottle.

He was too slow.

She screamed louder.

I thrust her into his arms and did it myself.

But it was too hot.

She screamed louder still.

I ran it under the tap to cool it down.

And still she screamed. Her face was purple with rage. I thought she was going to stop breathing.

By the time it was cool enough, she was in such a state she was hardly able to suck - pulling away from the teat to scream … refusing to take it.

I changed her nappy. Maybe it was that?

She screamed all through it.

I rocked her in my arms.

Giles tried to feed her.

She screamed.

He rocked her in *his* arms.

She screamed.

It took a very long time to give her that first bottle at home, and by the time it was done, all three of us were exhausted.

Little did we know that this was only the start of the screaming. It went on for weeks and months, day and night. It was ear-splitting. The only time it stopped was when one of us held her tightly against our body. She wouldn't lie in her cot, she would only sleep in our arms or lying on our chests and, even then, it wasn't long before she was screaming again. She seemed to need constant comfort.

Feeding her became a nightmare. A lot of the time she wouldn't feed at all. When she did, most of the milk would dribble down her chin. I was constantly washing her clothes and her bibs ... constantly worried that she was hungry, not getting enough nutrition. Her head was still very floppy, and I noticed that she always looked up and to the left. Her eyes would move around but always came to rest in the same position.

We couldn't understand what was wrong with her. I had begun to wonder if she was in pain. I asked the Health Visitor.

"She's just a crying baby, dear. Some of them are like that. Colicky."

Giles went back to work leaving me to cope on my own. I knew he had to, but it didn't stop me feeling as though he was deliberately avoiding the situation. He worked longer and longer hours, to "earn more overtime." He was never at home, and I felt angry and resentful towards him. I was drained and exhausted. I snapped at him whenever he got home. Consequently, he spent more and more time at work. Our relationship was fraying at the edges.

I felt so alone. Trapped in a waking nightmare of screaming, feeding and nappies. All our friends seemed to have disappeared. Rachel really sorted out the "boys" from the "men". She always has done. Some people gradually melted out of our lives, while others toughed it out along with us. We came to learn who our true friends were. Our lives would never be the same again. I was exhausted. I started to get headaches every day. I was tense and anxious all the time. I felt like a failure as a mother. What was wrong with me? What was wrong with Rachel?

I spent more and more time with my parents. I'd go over there every morning and return at night after Giles got back from work. I really needed and appreciated their help but, at the same time, I was conflicted about it. Relying on my parents just added to my feelings of failure and inadequacy as a mother.

They were constantly giving me advice: "Leave her to cry ... wind her more often ... hold the bottle at a different angle ... change the teat ... change the milk ... take her out in the pram ..."

None of it worked. She carried on screaming, and I felt as though they thought it was because of the way I was caring for her.

Giles' parents tried to help as much as they could, too. His mum cooked for us every Tuesday. Although I know they meant well, they were very overprotective. I felt smothered and even more stressed around them. It was easier to be with my own parents. One night, early on, they invited

Giles, Rachel and me, along with my mum and dad, round for dinner to celebrate Rachel's arrival. Rachel screamed continuously for the whole three hours we were there, and we spent the entire evening passing her from person to person as we tried to eat.

Our neighbour, Vicky, lived next door on one side and her parents on the other. Her parents' house was attached to ours, and I worried constantly that Rachel's crying would disturb them, especially at night, when it seemed louder than ever against the silence of the sleeping world. If it did, they never said a word. Even when I asked them, they denied it. I'll always be grateful for their kindness.

Vicky became a rock to me. She was always there when I needed to talk or have a break from it all. She listened and never judged. Never gave advice unless I asked for it. Her wisdom and quiet patience were some of the things that got me through those first difficult weeks and months.

Although it was tough, it wasn't all bad. There were short interludes when Rachel slept, and even some spells when she didn't cry. The one thing that she really loved was music. She loved me to sing to her and dance with her in my arms. When my dad sang 'The Grand Old Duke of York' to her, she would stop crying for a while as if she was mesmerised by the sounds and rhythm.

When Rachel was four weeks old, my mother came with me to take her for her EEG test. I didn't really know what to expect. I felt anxious and uncomfortable about taking my tiny, newborn baby into the big, teaching hospital in the centre of the city. She seemed so small and vulnerable. People were hurrying about in all directions. There seemed to be hundreds of signs pointing to hundreds of different wards and departments. Patients pushing drip-stands wandered about in hospital dressing gowns and slippers. It smelt of disinfectant with an undertone of dust and decay.

We found the Neurology Department, where we were shown into a cubicle and asked to lay Rachel on a couch. Its red plastic covering was cracked and peeling. The whole place seemed dingy and tired. I wondered who had lain on this couch before her. I spent so much time at home keeping her clean, sterilising her bottles and equipment, washing her clothes and bedding.

I covered the surface with her blanket before I laid her down. She started to scream. They glued electrodes to her head and connected them to a machine. She screamed even louder. I tried to give her a dummy, but she spat it out and it fell onto the floor. I stuffed it into my pocket. I'd have to sterilise it before she could have it again. They didn't say anything about the test. They said that Rachel's doctor would talk to us about the results.

Two weeks later, when Rachel was six weeks old, Giles and I took her for her follow-up appointment with her paediatrician. As soon as I saw the little, grey-haired woman again, I remembered the first time we had met her on Special Care, when she had told us that Rachel might not survive the night. It seemed like a lifetime ago. I hadn't ever looked at her properly back then, I was so distressed. It struck me now that she was really quite old - probably nearing retirement.

We were taken into an examination room. Rachel was screaming as usual. There were several medical students crowded into the small space. They were all looking at Rachel and the doctor, seemingly intent on her every word. She examined Rachel on a couch and asked how she was getting on. We told her about the screaming and the feeding and about how she looked up and to the left all the time. She gave Rachel back to me and sat down.

"Well, I have some good news, and some bad news, I'm afraid."

We looked at each other. Thankfully, Rachel had stopped screaming. It was as if she knew this was an important moment.

"The good news is that she doesn't have epilepsy."

We waited.

"The bad news is that Rachel has suffered some sort of brain damage."

Chapter Six – The Aftermath

I couldn't speak, but a million questions were rushing through my head.

The doctor was still talking.

" … happens to some babies … "

What did she mean? Brain damage?

" … never going to win on Sports Day … "

How could this have happened?

"… take her home and dress her prettily …"

But she was perfect. Beautiful. How could she have brain damage?

" … give her plenty of love …"

How would this affect her?

" … support when you need it …"

What did this mean for her? For us?

" ... see you again in four weeks ..."

We left the room in a state of stunned silence, with all our questions unasked.

We didn't speak on the way home, both lost in our own thoughts. Giles stared at the road ahead. His hands gripped the steering wheel. The muscles in his face twitched but his jaw was tightly clenched. I stared out of the window trying to think. Rachel was crying again. I tried to block out the sound while I attempted to make sense of what we had just heard.

What did she mean? How could she be sure? She looked perfect. It must be a mistake. We couldn't label our beautiful little girl as "brain-damaged". What would that mean for her future?

But, then again, the crying, the feeding problems, the way her eyes turned to the left all the time. Maybe she was right?

We spoke to our parents. Their reaction was the same as ours. Disbelief! Denial! Confusion! Distress! Fear!

A day or two later, the Health Visitor came to visit. I asked her about something the paediatrician had said that had been playing on my mind ... something about Rachel's soft spot closing early.

She frowned, and then looked concerned.

"No, no! If the soft spot closes now, the brain will have no room to grow."

She looked at Rachel for a long moment. She looked at the cot, which Rachel never slept in.

"Didn't they give you an apnoea mattress? She could still stop breathing and how would you know?"

Already tired and emotional, the encounter had tipped me over the edge. By the time she left, I was hysterical. I was losing control. I had worked myself into a complete panic. I called my mum, garbling out all my fears and anxieties in a rush of tearful, broken sentences and phrases. When she'd managed to get me to slow down and was able to understand some of what I was saying, she suggested I rang the GP.

The GP was calming and helpful. She reassured me that the whole "soft spot" thing didn't make any sense, and that maybe I had misunderstood somehow. Of course, Rachel's brain would continue to grow. And if the hospital thought that Rachel should have an apnoea mattress, they would have given her one.

When I put down the phone I felt better ... calmer. But, deep inside, I was still anxious and afraid. More anxious than I had ever been in my life - anxious and very confused. How could this be happening to me … to us? I had a great life. I was healthy, strong and successful. I was surrounded by a loving family and friends. I had married a man who truly loved me, and I loved him. How could everything have gone so wrong, so quickly?

Later that day, Rachel smiled properly for the first time. It was the sweetest smile I had ever seen. It lit up her whole face. It made my aching heart soar. How could someone with brain damage smile like this? They had to have made a mistake.

An appointment came through for Rachel's routine six-week check. She would actually be eight weeks old when it took place. It was at the Child Health Clinic in town.

I don't really know why, but when we were there, I decided not to tell the doctor what I had been told about Rachel. Maybe I wanted to test them? Maybe I wanted to see if what I had been told was true? Maybe another doctor would think that Rachel was perfectly healthy, and this would all go away? But I was honest about her history: the birth, Special Care, the crying, the feeding and the looking to the left.

Who was I kidding? The doctor looked more and more serious as she examined Rachel. When she finished her examination, she turned to me with a somber expression.

"I'm so sorry but I have grave concerns about how Rachel is developing. I'm going to have to refer her back to the paediatrician who looked after her while she was in hospital."

Reality began to sink in. If that doctor could tell things were not right after just one short examination, it must be bad. I was beginning to accept that what I had been told was true.

But with acceptance came questions. Questions about reasons, possible causes and explanations. Questions with no answers. Questions and guilt. I was full of guilt. Convinced that it was all my fault - that it must be due to something I had done.

I went over and over the pregnancy in my mind. What had I done wrong? I had done everything an expectant mother should do to look after herself and her baby. I'd read all the books. Followed all the advice I had been given by the midwives and doctors. I couldn't think of anything.

I wasn't the only one looking for answers … assigning blame. My dad suggested that I might have drunk too much orange juice during the pregnancy. Apparently, he'd been speaking to the grandmother of another baby in Special Care and that was what had caused the problem in their case. Giles' dad was convinced that I had spent too much time sitting in front of the gas fire, and that the fumes had permeated into the baby's brain. Although I knew it was ridiculous, the fact that they were looking to me, and something I had done, as the cause of the problem merely added to my misery.

I was also embarrassed. I didn't like being the centre of attention … didn't like everybody feeling sorry for me and constantly asking how we were coping and how I was feeling. I started to brush away people's questions. Of course, we were coping. Why wouldn't we be? Everything was fine.

But it wasn't. It wasn't fine at all. I was exhausted and heartbroken - the proverbial emotional wreck. Every day was a struggle. I was surviving on just a few hours' sleep. I couldn't talk to anyone. Giles was struggling with his own emotions. He too was looking for answers. I felt desperately alone. I had nowhere to turn.

But through it all, I was beginning to wonder what I could do to help Rachel. The paediatrician had told us to dress her prettily and give her plenty of love, but *anyone* would do that for *any* baby. She had not given me any specific advice on how to care for *Rachel*. Rachel was going to need *more* help and support than other baby, not less. There must be more that I could do for her. There had to be. But I had no idea where to start.

At our next appointment with the paediatrician, things continued in the same vein. She examined Rachel again and conducted a few developmental tests. This time she seemed particularly concerned about her eyesight, commenting that she was still continually looking to the left, and didn't seem to be actually looking at anything or anyone, or following objects with her eyes. But when I asked if Rachel could be blind, she was very non-committal. She seemed reluctant to refer her to an eye specialist, saying that it was too early to worry about things like that. Again, she offered us no explanation as to what might have caused Rachel's brain damage and no advice about what, if anything, we could to do help her.

And so, the nightmare continued. I felt trapped in a never-ending cycle of long, difficult days and, even longer, sleepless nights. I had always tried my best to make sure that Giles got his rest at night, but now he was working weekends and night shifts to earn even more money. I often had to try not to disturb him during the day, as well as at night. I had no chance to catch up on my own sleep as I was alone with Rachel all day, every day. I didn't feel there was anyone I could turn to for help - anyone I could ask to look after her for me for a while to give me break. It just seemed too much to ask of anyone. There was no end to it. It was relentless.

But I continued to pretend that everything was fine, and that I was managing perfectly well thank you, when inside I was screaming ... screaming for help, for some relief, for just a moment of release from it all.

Over time, the feelings of fear and anxiety, grief and distress, and guilt and embarrassment, were joined by something different, but equally as painful. All my life I had been as free as a bird. Since I was a small child, I had been raised to be strong and independent. I was allowed to roam and play outside, coming and going as I wished. My parents encouraged me to make my own choices and decisions, and to stand by them. This was what had helped shape me into the woman I had become. But now, I found myself in a situation in which I had no choice. I felt trapped and constrained, almost claustrophobic - totally helpless and out of control. There seemed to be nothing I could to do help myself, and nothing I could do to help Rachel.

I descended into a very dark place. I was overwhelmed by exhaustion and self-pity. Why had this happened to me? It wasn't fair. I'd done nothing to deserve it.

For a while, I turned to God for help. I prayed for

Him to help me. I prayed for Him to heal Rachel's brain, to make her whole again. I bargained with Him, promising to be a better person if He would just make her better.

Around this time, Giles' mother reminded me that we had said we would ask the vicar who christened Rachel in the hospital, to perform a blessing ceremony, one that the whole family could attend. It was perfect timing. It seemed to be exactly what I needed … exactly what Rachel needed … what we all needed.

I called the vicar excitedly to ask him. I couldn't wait to tell him that Rachel had survived that night, that she was still alive, and we were now ready to have the blessing he had promised us.

It was a short conversation.

While he said he was pleased to hear that Rachel had survived, he was unfortunately unable to perform the service as we lived outside his parish. He was sorry if he had misled me, but he was sure I would understand.

I was devastated! No, I didn't understand! I didn't understand at all! How could he be so cold - so heartless? Rachel had survived against all the odds, and now he was reneging on his promise. A promise that, at the time, had meant so much to me. He had clearly promised me anything that night, because he didn't believe that Rachel was going to survive and that he would actually have to keep his word. It clearly meant nothing to him and learning this rendered the christening he had performed in the hospital meaningless.

I stopped praying to God after that. In fact, I never prayed again. No one was going to help me with this. Not God, nor man. I had to find the strength from within.

I think I turned a corner that day. I stopped feeling sorry for myself and started to try and take back some control over my life. I began to think about things I could do myself to help Rachel, instead of waiting for advice and support that never seemed to come.

I started by working out how I could go back to work. I urgently needed some downtime to preserve my sanity. My parents ran the family business from their home. This was the same business I had worked in before Rachel was born. My mum and auntie agreed to do a job share with me. Throughout the day, we all took turns to look after Rachel for an hour or two. It was a small step, but it made an enormous difference to my life.

When Rachel was about three months old, a work colleague of Giles, Richard, and his wife, Christine, came to visit us. They had a daughter with severe brain damage. It felt wonderful to be able to talk to people who understood what we were going through. I bombarded them with questions. I shared all my feelings of guilt, frustration, and helplessness with them, and drew great comfort from the fact that they had experienced all the same emotions.

They told us about their daughter, Alice, and the time she had been admitted to hospital at 18 months old with uncontrollable seizures. The doctors in their local hospital had been unable to stop them and had called in the assistance of another doctor from Birmingham. Dr. G. had arrived and got the situation under control in less than an hour. Since then, he had taken over the management of Alice's care. They couldn't speak highly enough of him.

They gently suggested to me that they suspected Rachel was having frequent small seizures. I had noticed that her fingers twitched from time to time but had not thought this was of any significance. They said they were sure that this was a sign she was having a seizure, as they had seen it before in Alice. They suggested that perhaps we should try to get a referral for Rachel with Dr. G.

After they left, I got straight on the phone to my GP. At last, it felt like there was something I could do. We were still seeing Rachel's paediatrician every four weeks, but every appointment went the same way. An examination, followed by a brief conversation about what Rachel was and wasn't doing, and how we were coping. Never any advice about what we could do to help her.

Through the GP, I made an appointment to see Dr. G. in October, when Rachel would be five months old. I made it privately as his NHS waiting list was exceptionally long, and I wanted her to see him as soon as possible. It felt so good to be doing something proactive at last - something positive and constructive.

Chapter Seven – Learning to Cope

We met Dr. G. in his office at the rear of the Children's Hospital. The room was chaotic. Books and journals on child health were strewn all over the place. Files and paperwork covered every surface. He listened attentively as we explained why we were there. He asked us a few questions, and then he spoke to Rachel.

No-one had ever done that before. Her paediatrician, the GP, the doctor who did the six-week examination, and the health visitor had all spoken about Rachel, and spoken to us about her, but none of them had ever spoken directly to her. I liked him straight away, and my headache began to clear.

He went on to examine her. As he stood up to undertake his examination, I couldn't help but notice that he was wearing odd socks. I liked him even more.

He laid her gently on his examination couch and measured her head circumference and tested her reflexes, talking to her quietly all the time. She seemed remarkably calm through all of this.

When he was finished, he sat down and talked to us again. He said that he was going to arrange for Rachel to see an eye specialist, a developmental specialist, and a physiotherapist. He also wanted her to have another EEG as he suspected that our friends' fears about her having frequent small seizures were correct.

At the end of the consultation he turned to Rachel and said, "You've been a very good little girl."

By the time we left his office I was elated. We had set up all the appointments with his secretary. Other than the one with the eye specialist, they were all on the same day at the same hospital. We had also settled our bill for the private appointment and were even more impressed when we were asked to make the cheque out to a local children's charity.

Finally, someone we felt we could trust was going to help us. Finally, it felt as though things were happening that were going to make a difference for Rachel. Things that might help her overcome some of the challenges that she was going to have to face. Things that involved more than dressing her prettily and giving her lots of love. There were no words to express how hopeful and grateful we already were for the help and support Dr. G. was offering us.

Things were beginning to improve in other ways, too. The nights were still tough, but the days were getting easier. The crying was less. Rachel was doing more: smiling and looking around and responding to different types of stimulation. We started to venture out more: day trips to the zoo, or to the butterfly farm in Stratford-on-Avon, followed by a walk along the banks of the river. Rachel enjoyed these days, and so did we. It was such a pleasure to be doing things like other people did with their young families.

Even feeding was improving. Rachel loved her food, and now that she was able to eat solids, we began to experiment with different flavours and textures. She took everything we offered her with a joyful enthusiasm and a great deal of mess. Chocolate pudding was one of her favourites. Swallowing was still difficult for her, but she would splutter and choke her way through it, until we were both splattered from head to toe in chocolate.

On one memorable crisp and cool morning, my mum was trying to entertain Rachel by theatrically slurping the cup of tea she was drinking. Mum had just let out a particularly impressive "slurp", when, out of the blue, Rachel started to laugh. Her face lit up with amusement and her whole body shook as she let out a long hearty chuckle.

I was thrilled. I slurped my own tea and she laughed again. Mum laughed at her laughing, and she laughed even more. I joined in and, for a few precious moments, the three of us laughed as if we didn't have care in the world. I was overjoyed. My baby could laugh.

A week or so after we saw Dr. G., we met with the eye specialist, Mr. W., another delightful and charming man, with a reassuringly old-fashioned "bedside manner". He was certain that Rachel wasn't blind, which was wonderful news. He gave us some exercises to do at home to help strengthen her eye muscles. He also explained that she had a bilateral squint and that, at some point, she would need surgery to correct this.

A few days later, we spent the whole day at the Children's Hospital for all the other appointments. The first was with the developmental specialist, Dr. C. He tried to get Rachel to perform a number of tasks that would be fairly easy for a baby of her age.

She couldn't grasp a toy that was placed in front of her. She couldn't hold a rattle that was placed in her hand. She couldn't follow bright objects with her eyes as he moved them from left to right in front of her. She couldn't push herself up with her arms when she was lying on her tummy. She couldn't hold her head up or sit unassisted.

It was disappointing and very upsetting for me to watch this as those were all tasks that I had been trying to teach Rachel over the previous few months and had witnessed my friend's baby master with ease.

But Rachel could smile, and she could laugh … and she did so, all through the assessment as he tried to get her to do one task after another. I could tell that she had won him over with her big cross-eyed smile and infectious laugh.

He felt that her physical delay was more marked than her intellectual one, and that her hearing seemed to be completely unaffected. It was a small thing, but something that was particularly important. I had already noticed her love of music and that she responded better to auditory stimulation than visual. This just confirmed what I had already worked out for myself, but it was going to be important in the future when we were working out the best way to communicate with her.

Following that, we had the physiotherapy assessment. By that point, Rachel was tired and irritable. She cried throughout the whole session. She objected loudly to every position the therapist tried to put her in. When she rolled her around on the top of a big ball, she nearly brought the roof down!

I knew it was important, as it would dictate what further support Rachel would receive in the future from our local physiotherapy service, but it was difficult to watch. The entire time, I had to stop myself from intervening and putting a stop to it all. It was so hard to see my baby girl in so much distress.

By the time we got to our last appointment of the day, the EEG, she was inconsolable. It was the same procedure as the last time, except for the fact that Rachel's hair had grown. She had developed a beautiful head of thick blond curls, that were sticky and matted together with electrode glue by the time we took her home that night, all of us miserable and exhausted. We were certain it would all be worth it, and it was wonderful to be finally getting some medical attention that was positive and constructive, but part of me wondered if she'd ever forgive us for what we'd put her through.

Soon after the physiotherapy assessment, we had our first appointment with LB, Rachel's community physiotherapist. The minute I met her, I knew she was going to be an important and positive force in our lives. She had a good energy about her and a twinkle in her eyes. She was warm and open, with a mane of thick blond hair piled miraculously on top of her head, and she fell in love with Rachel straight away. She ran through a series of exercises, similar to those that had been performed at the initial assessment. Rachel was just as unimpressed as she had been that day, but LB was undaunted. She cheerfully chatted away to her, calling her "honey", and rolling her around on a big stripy beach ball as Rachel screamed blue murder.

She told me that she would come and work with Rachel twice a week for an hour, but that, in between, I should do some exercises with her as often as I could. She went on to take me through what I needed to do, stressing how important this was for Rachel's physical development.

I started them as soon as she left. At last, I had a sense of purpose. A role to play in Rachel's care, other than feeding and changing her and rocking her in my arms when she cried. It was also the start of a close and very special relationship between myself and LB, who developed into someone I was able to talk to, other than family members, about my feelings around Rachel. I looked forward to her visits immensely.

It was a cold November morning when we went back to see Dr. G. for the results of all the tests and assessments. His office was still chaotic, and he was still wearing odd socks. I was fairly sure that he was wearing different coloured shoes as well.

Dr. C. had confirmed that Rachel had severe developmental delay. As we already knew, she was definitely going to need regular intensive physiotherapy. And, as suspected, the EEG had shown that she was having frequent small seizures and should start anti-epileptic medication right away. (With disgust, I remembered the paediatrican's "good news" that Rachel didn't have epilepsy, and my admiration for Dr. G. grew even more.)

There was a lot to take in, but it was all positive. We had a clearer idea of what some of Rachel's problems were, and what could be done to help her. At last, I felt that we were moving forward … taking action. It was a significant turning point in all our lives. But the most important thing of all that happened that day was that Rachel was finally given a diagnosis.

As well as everything else that Dr. G. explained to us that cold November morning, he told us that Rachel had a type of brain damage called Cerebral Palsy. I held Rachel even tighter in my arms, afraid of what this meant, afraid that I might lose her.

Cerebral Palsy. The words went round and round in my head.

I'd heard the term before but didn't really know what it meant. As soon as I could after we got home, I left Rachel with my mum and went to our local library to look it up. There was so much information, it was hard to make sense of it all. I scanned through the pages of countless medical textbooks.

The effects of the condition seemed to vary enormously depending on the severity of the brain damage. It was hard to know what was relevant to Rachel and what was not. Some of the pictures of children and young people with severe physical disabilities were deeply disturbing. As I studied the images, a cold chill washed over me.

Dr. G. had said that Rachel's condition was moderate to severe. He said that the chances of her ever being able to walk were small, but that the condition affected different people in different ways. He explained that we wouldn't know how she was affected intellectually until she was older. Sometimes people with severe physical disabilities were untouched intellectually, and equally people with severe intellectual problems could appear almost unaffected from a physical point of view.

As I sat in the silent library surrounded by piles of books, it gradually began to dawn on me for the very first time, that Rachel was definitely going to be disabled. But just how badly we would have to wait to find out. This was incredibly hard for me to accept and I wasn't making it any easier on myself by sitting in the library surrounded by shockingly graphic black and white images of children with her condition.

I had also asked Dr. G. what might have caused Rachel's condition and he had said it was most likely to be something that happened at birth, but that wasn't something to focus on at the moment. He said that, for now, we should focus all our energy on helping her to have the best life she could possibly have. While I wasn't entirely satisfied with his answer, I tried to follow his advice, but I still had many unanswered questions about her birth and what might have caused her cerebral palsy.

With everything that was going on, Christmas took me by complete surprise that year. It was only when some cards and gifts started to arrive for Rachel, that I realised how close it was.

We had made it to Rachel's first Christmas.

I thought back to those terrible weeks in May, when she was fighting for her life. I had never dared to think as far ahead as Christmas. But here we were. She was seven months old and thriving. As more and more gifts and cards arrived every day, we decided it was time to celebrate. It was comforting — something else to focus on — and I threw myself into the preparations.

One evening, Giles brought home the tree. We decorated it with little toy soldiers, tiny ballerinas and white fairy lights. I sat Rachel on my knee to watch as Giles switched on the lights. She was enchanted. Her face lit up and she laughed with delight. Then, overcome with excitement, she kicked her legs for the very first time.

Sitting in front of that beautiful tree, with Rachel on my lap, giggling and smiling and kicking her little legs in glee, was the best Christmas present of my life. I didn't only have a star on top of my tree, I had a little star on my lap, too.

Christmas came and went, and in January we decided to take our first holiday together. We didn't feel brave enough to take Rachel on a plane yet, and concerns about her health were always front of mind for us. We never knew when she might have some sort of crisis that would require emergency care. So, we rented a self-catering holiday lodge on the Isle of Wight. It wasn't too far away if we decided we couldn't cope and needed help from our parents or wanted to go back home.

The lodge was lovely, but the island didn't quite live up to our expectations of a family-oriented holiday destination. There wasn't much to do, and none of the pubs or restaurants were geared up for children in those days. In fact, we never managed to find a pub that even allowed us all in. It felt so good to get away, though. Rachel adored having Mummy and Daddy's undivided attention all day, every day, and we felt as if we had left all our problems behind us, even though it was for just a short while. Nobody there knew who we were and what we were going through. With her beautiful blue eyes, blond curls and chubby face, Rachel looked like any other healthy baby. When we were out and about, people would stop to admire her and fuss over her.

The new year brought a new structure and routine into my life with Rachel, and with it a new positivity. As well as doing her physio several times a day, I made sure she had her medication. The drug Dr. G. had prescribed was called clonazepam. It came in a tablet form but, because of her swallowing difficulties, I had to crush it and mix it with honey to ensure that she took it.

Having a baby with multiple additional and special needs had been a rapid and uncompromising introduction to adulthood and the responsibilities of being a parent. But I was coping. Somehow, I had stepped up to the plate and was taking it all in my stride. Looking back, it was a time of dramatic transformation for me.

Don't get me wrong. Things were getting better, but they still weren't perfect by any means. I still had my ups and downs. I still felt lonely and isolated. It was difficult to maintain the friendships I had before. Most people couldn't cope with what we were going through and just drifted away. It was difficult for me to spend time with friends who had babies of their own. I couldn't stop myself from comparing what their babies could do, with what Rachel could not.

I had one particular friend who had been pregnant at the same time as me. We got together from time to time during our babies' first six months. I found it so painful watching her baby grow and develop. She seemed to have learned something new every time I saw her. My friend constantly asked me questions about Rachel. Why can't she do this? Why does she do that?

This friend also happened to work with Giles' mother. For reasons only she will ever understand, one day she chose to tell me about his mum's reaction when she took some of her baby photos into work. Giles' mum had apparently looked wistfully at the pictures and said that she would be too ashamed to show her colleagues pictures of Rachel.

I couldn't understand this reaction from my mother-in-law, because, when I gazed at photos of Rachel, all I saw was my daughter's beauty and all I felt was pride.

The final straw for the friendship came when I was invited to her daughter's christening, only to discover that the same vicar who had refused to bless Rachel was performing the ceremony, despite the fact that they *also* lived outside his area. I was devastated. I didn't see her much after that.

My best friend, Louise, lived in Switzerland at this time. Louise and I went right back. We met at school when we were just eight years old and were inseparable from then on. Well, inseparable that was, until her family moved to Switzerland when we were both ten. We kept in touch though, travelling back and forth between Switzerland and the UK, and spending all our summers together. She remains my closest friend to this day, even though she now lives in the USA.

She had flown over for a brief visit soon after Rachel was born. But because Rachel was still in Special Care, we'd not really been able to spend much time together. At the time, she had just discovered that she was pregnant with her first child. Her little boy, Neil, was born in the December, so she, too, was now a new mum. I missed her terribly. We spent hours on the phone and spoke most weeks, but it wasn't the same as seeing each other face to face. I really wanted her to get to know Rachel, and vice versa.

Looking back, she never made me feel bad like the other friends who had babies made me feel. I don't remember how she did it, but she never seemed to draw me into making comparisons between Neil and Rachel. She was, and always will be, a true friend to Rachel and me.

While things were getting easier in many ways, and we were learning to cope with our new way of life, I was also becoming aware that Giles and I were drifting apart as a couple. I was totally absorbed in caring for Rachel and doing her exercises, and Giles continued to work long hours to support us. When he got home, he would take over with the exercises, while I had a bath and then cooked dinner. While I was cooking, he would bathe her. Rachel loved her bath, and this developed into a special time for them. As soon as she heard the key in the lock, she would look towards the door. When I told her "Daddy's home", her face would light up and she would strain to watch for him coming into the room.

But Giles and I never spent any quality time alone together. Rachel still didn't sleep well and by now we were taking alternate nights to stay up with her. We were both exhausted all the time and never slept in the same bed together. When Rachel was awake, all our attention was focused on her, and when she slept, we slept, anxious to make the most of the opportunity.

I tried not to think about it, telling myself it would all work out when she was older. It was only natural that she was our priority at the moment. We were still learning how to care for her - still getting used to it. Things were getting better all the time. We'd be alright. We loved each other. We were a strong couple. We'd get through this and get back to where we were. Or, so I hoped.

S.J. Gibbs & J.M. McKenzie

Chapter Eight – A Fresh Start

Early in 1988, Giles and I agreed that we wanted to try and make a fresh start. Slowly but surely, the layers of shock were peeling away, enabling us to see more clearly, and deal more pragmatically, with the hard facts of our lives with Rachel in them.

We decided to move to a new house, somewhere slightly bigger and more suited to our new way of life. The sale went through quickly, and we moved in the March. The house was close to both of our parents and gave us more space to accommodate Rachel's ever-growing needs. She had a bigger bedroom with extra storage for all her equipment, and a double bed, so that whichever one of us was on "night duty" could sleep beside her. The house was also detached, which made her night crying easier to deal with.

And so, we settled into our new routine. The

weekdays were busy. I spent most of my time at my mum's, as I was still job-sharing, and care-sharing, with my mum and aunt. The arrangement worked perfectly for us all. My aunt was amazing with Rachel, and with me. She was extremely supportive and caring, and I could see the genuine love and concern she had for us in her eyes. The arrangement meant that there was always someone caring for Rachel. My mum and my aunt felt that they were helping, and I got regular breaks. It also enabled me to maintain a job and still attend the numerous hospital and physiotherapy appointments that Rachel's condition demanded.

At weekends we tried to get out and about as much as possible. Rachel loved being outdoors in her pushchair and, when the weather was fine, we would go for long walks together. Stratford-on-Avon was still one of our favourite spots. She would kick her legs in delight as we strolled along the riverside or stopped to feed the ducks. Sometimes, we hired a rowing boat and took her out on the river. Seeing how much joy she got from these trips made it an enjoyable experience for us, too.

We all worked hard on her physio. There was barely a moment, apart from when she was eating or sleeping, that someone wasn't going through her exercises with her. Twice a week, I stayed home for LB's visits. We really looked forward these sessions. I loved getting involved with all the exercises, and even Rachel seemed to be beginning to enjoy them. We still did a lot of work with the big ball. LB would sit Rachel on top of it and hold her in position as she rolled the ball from side to side. This was to help develop her head control and balance. Even though she found the exercises hard and tiring at times, she never complained or gave up. It was during these sessions that her courage and strength first began to shine through for me.

LB also gave us a corner seat with high sides and a pommel in the middle, specially designed to support Rachel in a sitting position. Giles made her a little table to put in front of the seat. We would put her toys and books on it, so that she could see them. She couldn't grasp them, but she loved to look at them with us. Giles also built her another table at standing height, which we used to do standing exercises to strengthen her legs. I would sit behind her and place her arms on the table, so that she could support some of her weight. She needed my help to balance but could maintain the position for a few minutes.

Sometimes though, it felt as though we were putting in such a lot of effort for little or no improvement in Rachel's physical development. But with LB's constant motivation and encouragement, I always felt better after she'd been. She was someone I could rely on to answer my questions as truthfully as she could.

My father was emerging as Rachel's hero during

this time. Whenever he came into the room, he would rescue her from whoever was taking her through her exercises, by scooping her up in his arms and dancing and singing to her. She would reward him with peals of laughter or a beaming smile.

LB taught me a lot about Cerebral Palsy. One afternoon she arranged a session for the whole family to talk us through it. She explained that Rachel's nervous system had been damaged in such a way that her brain didn't understand the messages it was receiving from her body. She said we should try and think of it like a radio station that wasn't properly tuned in. Rachel's brain was still receiving signals from all five of her senses, but these messages were confused, and her brain couldn't make her body respond to them in the way that it should. Nobody had described it in this way before, and it gave us all a better understanding of how Rachel's brain and body were working.

For example, Rachel might want to move her arm to reach out and touch something, but her brain could not send the correct signals to the muscles in order for her to do that. Because Rachel's muscles could not respond properly to her brain's signals, they didn't work properly and became tight and shortened, leading to the spasticity that is so common in all people with cerebral palsy. This was why the physiotherapy was so important.

While it increased my understanding as to why she couldn't do certain things, and how to help her, it also seemed so cruel and unfair that her brain was unable to get its vital messages to her body. It broke my heart.

Around this time, Rachel also started having speech therapy. When she was excited, Rachel would open her mouth wide and it would stick in that position as her muscles went into spasm. So, at this stage, it was more about training and strengthening her mouth muscles, than actually about her speech, and involved lots of different mouth exercises.

Like the physiotherapy sessions, these sessions took place at our house, but they were not as enjoyable as LB's visits for Rachel, nor for me. To me, the speech therapist seemed to have limited knowledge of cerebral palsy and limited patience with Rachel. I would watch the clock during her sessions, anxious for them to be over and for it to be time for her to leave.

Feeding and eating were the domain of the speech therapist, and she insisted that we try all sorts of different approaches to mealtimes. As a result, feeding Rachel, which had never been easy, was rapidly becoming a nightmare. We were to stop pureeing all Rachel's food and try her with foods of different textures that required her to chew. We were also to try to help her feed herself. It felt as though all the speech therapist did was dole out a long list of instructions without ever considering how difficult they were going to be for us to implement.

At mealtimes, I had to sit beside her and put her food on her table while she sat in her chair. Then, I had to place my hand over hers and try to help her to feed herself with a spoon. Her drinks were to be given to her in an orange plastic cup with two handles. Again, I was to place my hands over hers and try to help her to drink from the cup. Mealtimes were a disaster. They went on forever. Food and drink seemed to go everywhere but into Rachel's mouth. I worried that she wasn't getting the nourishment she needed. I was frustrated and upset.

But Rachel loved her food, and I hid my feelings from her and tried to be patient. I began to dread every meal and they seemed to come around more and more quickly. I persevered, believing it would help her in the long run, but for many years, these times were difficult for me. Sometimes, I despised myself for finding feeding Rachel such a chore.

Rachel still loved music. In fact, she loved noise in general. Her favourite toys were ones that made a noise. The louder the better. She began to enjoy TV, especially the music programmes. Top of the

Pops became a weekly ritual for us.

Her love of sound extended to machines. She loved it when I turned on the food mixer I used to make her milk shakes. She liked sitting in front of the washing machine or tumble dryer, and the vacuum cleaner sent her into a frenzy of sheer delight. She nearly choked with laughter if my mum put the suction hose against her clothes.

I loved to sing to her and dance with her, and she adored it, too. She would kick her legs and smile and chuckle through every song. I used to sing one particular song to her a lot - *Where do you go to my lovely?* by Peter Sarstedt. The words held special meaning for me. They seemed to express exactly what I wanted to say to her.

Where do you go to my lovely, when you're alone in your bed? Tell me the thoughts that surround you. I want to look inside your head.

It still hurt that she couldn't play like other babies her age. She couldn't take her toys out of her toy box and scatter them around the house. I had to do that for her. Apart from mealtimes, she never got dirty or messy. I had to do that for her, too. I bought some finger paints and dipped her fingers in the paint and then onto the paper for her. I sat her in front of a mirror and smeared her paint-covered finger on the end of her nose. It broke my heart that she would never be able to do this for herself. She deserved more than anybody to be happy, and I was determined that she would be.

Time passed, and we learned to cope. We started to do things that normal families did. We had Sunday lunch, or "Nanny's dinner" as we called it for Rachel, at my parents' home every week. Every Tuesday, we had dinner at Giles' parents' house. It became a routine which suited us all. It meant we didn't have to worry about cooking twice a week. Both sets of grandparents enjoyed spending time with Rachel, and Giles and I could enjoy our meals without having to try and feed Rachel at the same time or have her perched on one of our laps.

We went on another holiday, this time venturing overseas to Majorca, where Rachel discovered her love of swimming. She had no fear of the water and loved floating and splashing about in the pool as one of us supported her. I think it gave her a freedom of movement that she had never experienced before. In fact, hydrotherapy went on to become an important part of her treatment in the future. The holiday was a huge success and a wonderful experience for all three of us.

Despite my disillusionment with God, and the church in general - and mainly for the grandparents' sakes - we went ahead and arranged a blessing ceremony for her. I had a gown made for her from my wedding dress and bought her a white lacy bonnet and booties to match. She looked beautiful and it was a wonderful day. I have to admit that the vicar did a great job, but, while his words were sensitive and comforting, they failed to resolve my ongoing problems with the church in general.

We had a big party after the ceremony. Louise came over from Switzerland to be a godparent along with her husband. Rachel loved every minute of it. She adored parties and all the fuss and attention she got. She still does to this day.

Soon after we moved into the new house, I discovered, completely coincidentally, that another family with a child with cerebral palsy lived next door. I was reading an article about a local family who were raising money for their son, when I realised that they were our neighbours.

I was euphoric. This was meant to be. I would have someone to share all my challenges with, and Rachel would have a little friend. I couldn't wait to meet them. We would be able to help and support one another.

As soon as I could, we went round and introduced ourselves to them. But I was a little surprised by the mother's reaction. She didn't seem as excited to meet me as I was to meet her.

Her son was six months older than Rachel, and it appeared that she had had some difficult experiences. She seemed bitter and resentful. She told me that, like her son, Rachel was unlikely ever to be accepted by the local community. She described how people would cross the road if she met them in the street, rather than have to stop and speak to them.

I'll be honest, I'd expected her to say how cute Rachel was and all sorts of other nice things about her, like everyone else who met her did, but she barely acknowledged her. I was disappointed and a little shocked. So far, I had never experienced anything like she had described. It made me wonder what the future had in store for us. So far, my experience had been quite the opposite. Rachel was such a pretty, happy and smiling baby that people went out of their way to stop and admire her. Maybe it would be different as she got older and her disabilities became more apparent. I clearly had a lot more to learn about living with disability. I came away from the meeting feeling naïve and a little immature.

So, we never really hit it off with the neighbours, and things got even worse when, a few months later, during one of LB's visits, the mother rang and asked if she could speak to her. I didn't take much notice of it at the time, but later that day LB phoned me and asked if, from then on, Rachel could have some of her sessions at my parents' house as the neighbour had complained that

Rachel seemed to be getting more attention than her son. It didn't matter, as we spent most of our time there anyway, and it meant my mum could get more involved with Rachel's treatment. Nevertheless, it did shock me, especially as the reason Rachel needed more support than her little boy was because she wasn't developing as well and as quickly as him. I considered taking it up with her but decided against it. It wasn't a battle I had either the will or the energy to enter into at that point in time.

We still had regular appointments with the paediatrician and Dr. G., and they were both pleased with Rachel's progress. Aside from her developmental delay and her physical disabilities, she was growing into a beautiful, happy and healthy baby. Her general health was excellent. The medication was controlling her epilepsy and somehow, despite the mealtime fiascos, she was growing and thriving. Dr. G. had said that she may be prone to chest infections but, so far, she had experienced none of these. I mentally crossed my fingers and allowed myself a glimmer of hope that her health would continue in this way.

We had registered with a new GP when we moved house and they invited us to the surgery for a new patient check-up. The new doctor warmed to Rachel right away. She seemed to know just how to handle her and how to communicate with her.

She explained that in the past she had specialised in cerebral palsy and, from then on, took a special interest in Rachel. She arranged for the local health visitor to call on us regularly and she too got on really well with Rachel. She was also a great listener and took the time to listen to all my anxieties and concerns, however small and unimportant. We were gradually being surrounded by a solid support network of people we could trust, and who we knew had Rachel's best interests at heart.

But despite it all I still felt alone.

It's hard to explain. There was no doubt that things were looking up, and I knew I should be thankful that we had so much support and so many people who cared about us, but at the end of the day it was us who were ultimately accountable for Rachel … only us who would be there for her every single day for the rest of her life. The enormity of the responsibility was terrifying.

And I had started to think about the future. Now that we were learning to cope with the present and were recovering from the shock of what had happened to us, I found myself thinking more and more about what was going to happen as Rachel got older. What would she be able to do for herself? Would she be able to go to school? Was she going to need care for the rest of her life? And the most frightening question of all, how much older would she get? Would her condition have an impact on how long she was likely to live?

I kept these thoughts inside. I didn't even dare to speak them out loud to myself, let alone to anyone else.

In fact, I kept most things to myself. Apart from Louise, I didn't really have meaningful conversations with anyone. Apart from a few hours each day at work, I didn't really interact with anyone other than Rachel and her therapists and doctors. I was totally enveloped inside the bubble that was my life with Rachel. All my waking hours were spent caring for her. Trying to do my best to give her the best chance I could.

On top of all of this, Giles and I both knew that our marriage was definitely in trouble. We barely spoke to each other unless it was about Rachel. We never spent time alone together. We didn't sleep together. We knew we were broken, but somehow, we also both knew that was how it had to be. Rachel's needs were greater and more important than our own.

Chapter Nine – First Birthday Blues

Rachel's first birthday was rapidly approaching.

As the weather got warmer, I would take a blanket out into the garden, and Rachel and I would lie there together in the sunshine. I'd strip her off and let her enjoy the freedom to move without the restraints of her nappy. The heat would help her tight muscles to relax. She'd gurgle and kick as she enjoyed the sights and sounds of the garden, and the warmth of the spring sun on her skin.

One particularly sunny afternoon, I lay on my back beside her gazing up at the clear blue sky dotted with fluffy white clouds. But my mind was elsewhere. I was thinking about Rachel's future and what her life expectancy might be. I was in love with my beautiful little girl. My life revolved around her. I couldn't imagine life without her, but I had no idea how long she would live and was afraid to find out. It was eating me up ... consuming my thoughts ... spoiling my enjoyment of the good times we were having together.

I resolved to ask the question at our next appointment with Dr. G. Whatever the answer was, I needed to know. I needed to know when my daughter was likely to die.

Dr. G. was pleased with her progress. He examined her, and we discussed how her physio and speech therapy were going. He'd just begun to talk about when the right time might be for her eye surgery, but I couldn't hold it in any longer.

"Do you know how long Rachel is likely to live for?"

Giles looked at me in horror, but Dr. G. smiled.

"Oh, I'm sorry. Have we never discussed that?"

"No, we haven't," I replied.

"Well, no-one can ever really answer a question like that. Nothing is ever certain where life and death are concerned. But, in my view, Rachel can, to all intents and purposes, live a long and happy life."

I closed my eyes and let out a long sigh of relief.

"The evidence suggests that, because of her cerebral palsy, her life may be shortened by about

20 years compared to that of the average person. But again, even that is not certain. She will be prone to chest infections and her epilepsy could be a challenge, but with the proper care and attention, and good management of these issues, she should live well into late middle age, or even early old age."

I sat next to her in the car and kissed her all the way home. But my joy was short-lived. Now that I knew Rachel could possibly live a long life, I started to think even more about what the future might hold for us. I became obsessed with her development. I bought a book called 'Helping Your Handicapped Child'. It was like a big list of all the milestones that babies usually achieve at different ages. It was divided into three sections: motor, communication and social. Each section was sub-divided by month. I checked Rachel's skills against every milestone in every section. It was clear to me that Rachel was achieving most of the social skills that would be expected of a child of her age; it was the physical and communication sections where she was way behind.

I was determined to help her catch up. I noted the specific skills that we needed to prioritise. I would set goals and targets, and work on these until we achieved them, then tick them off with an enormous sense of pride and satisfaction. Some things took longer than others. I knew that she needed to sit before she could try to stand or walk, but we had been working on sitting unaided for six months and were making absolutely no progress.

It was gradually dawning on me that there were some things that Rachel was never going to be able to do. If she couldn't sit, she would never be able to stand or walk. She couldn't use her hands to pick things up or hold them. She couldn't respond to instructions to close her eyes or stick out her tongue. She couldn't make any properly formed sounds, other than what sounded like, car and nan, and I had to face the real possibility that she would never be able to talk.

LB tried to motivate me and cheer me up by showing me little things that had improved, like her hand tension. At six months, her hands had both been tight little fists but now her fingers were more relaxed, and her hands were even open for some of the time.

It didn't really help. Terror was building deep inside me as I realised the extent of Rachel's disability. I was becoming more and more depressed and despondent. But I couldn't show it. I had to keep these destructive feelings locked away inside. I felt guilty for having them.

Being around other people was hard. It brought up a whole raft of negative thoughts and emotions that I couldn't allow to come to the surface. It was so much easier when it was just Rachel and me.

My parents were an amazing support to me. They were not getting any younger, and some of the physical stuff was hard for them, but Mum helped with Rachel's exercises every day, and whenever Dad got home from work, he would whisk her up into his arms and dance and sing to her, prompting the usual smiles and peals of laughter.

She adored him. But I still felt guilty. They didn't mean to make me feel that way, I knew. But I couldn't bear to see the hurt and pain etched on their faces as they watched their little granddaughter's head lolling on her shoulders, or they wiped her face as most of her drink dribbled down her chin. I could see it in their faces …. the disappointment. I felt responsible. I had let them down.

With Giles' parents, it was even worse. They didn't agree with the physiotherapy and felt she shouldn't be forced to do her exercises. They didn't think it mattered … that it would make any difference. They were in the "dress her up pretty and give her lots of love" camp. I knew they still blamed me for what had happened to her. I could see the unspoken questions in their eyes: what could I have done so wrong for this to have happened to my baby - their grandchild?

I was also struggling to deal with the feeling that

people felt sorry for us. I didn't want their pity ... didn't need it. But this was mixed with a confusing sense of gratitude when people were nice to us, or even spent time with us and treated us normally. What was wrong with me?

On one occasion, the friend with the baby the same age as Rachel came over for tea. She suggested that the girls have a bath together ... that it might be fun for them.

Rachel loved it, but I was on the verge of tears the entire time. It hurt so much to see her daughter sitting and playing contentedly in the water, while I had to constantly support Rachel's head.

I was filled with gratitude that she had allowed us to share this experience and kept thanking her but didn't know why. But when she said, "It's alright. I know. Some people might not have let their baby share a bath with Rachel in case they caught a disease," her words stung me. I understood, but after they left, I cried for hours.

Even buying her first pair of shoes was an ordeal. LB had decided that Rachel needed some special shoes. She had ordered her some little, lace up, Piedro orthopaedic boots, to support her feet and ankles and keep her toes straight. They were not what I'd had in mind when I'd imagined my little girl's first pair of shoes. I'd imagined a pair of shiny, black patent ones, and I decided that she was still going to have them. So, I took Rachel to the shoe shop in town to have her feet measured.

"But she needs to stand up to have her feet measured."

The assistant was getting frustrated with me.

"But I told you. She can't stand," I said for the third time.

"We don't advise shoes for children who can't stand. They should really be walking before they start wearing shoes."

"Yes, but ... as I said, she can't walk, and she can't stand. The shoes are just for her to ... look pretty."

"I'll have to ask the manageress. Can you just wait there for a minute?"

The manageress arrived and I explained it all over again. The assistant was now looking at Rachel with a mixture of pity and fascination. I just wanted to get the shoes and get out of there.

Thankfully, the manageress was more understanding. She said she had to advise us against buying shoes without a proper fitting in case it damaged her feet, but as long as she would only be wearing them for short periods of time, she was sure it would be fine.

Rachel left the shop wearing a beautiful pair of shiny, black patent leather shoes. That night, and for many nights after, our song of choice was, "These boots are made for walking".

But we both grew to like her Piedro boots, too. They actually looked really cute on her little feet, and I knew they were good for her. But we both loved the shiny, black shoes that she saved for special occasions.

I was becoming fiercely protective of Rachel and becoming frustrated and irrational with anyone I didn't perceive as being on her side or prepared to make her their number one priority.

My parents had a little black poodle called Mitzy. She was a rescue dog and we'd had her since I was 12 and my brother was 3. She was part of the family. As Mitzy got older, she became smelly and incontinent, as all old dogs do. My mum was fastidious about clearing up her "mess", but, as Rachel spent a lot of her time on the floor, I became concerned that she was going to pick up an infection. I persuaded my parents that it was time to have Mitzy put to sleep.

They were horrified initially, but eventually agreed to do it for Rachel's sake. I knew it was the right thing to do but it didn't stop this from adding to the burgeoning mountain of guilt I was already carrying. My brother, Den, was devasted. I'm not sure he has ever forgiven me.

And so, every day, I would put on my "fine face". This was the face I showed to the world, but inside, I was lower than I'd ever been. I could feel myself spiralling downwards, faster and faster, as if I were being pulled into a vortex. Every night I would cry myself to sleep.

I thought I was hiding my inner feelings so well, but I was kidding myself. People had noticed that I wasn't looking after myself. I never put makeup on, nor had my hair done or bought any new clothes. When I look back at photos and videos of that time, I look way older than my 23 years.

My mum took me aside one day and asked me how I was. She said that someone had commented that I'd lost my bubble. I told her not to be silly. I was fine. But I knew she was right. I couldn't remember the last time I had laughed out loud.

LB was worried about me, too. She tried to cheer me up by telling me about a playgroup that Rachel might be able to go to when she was older. It was for babies and young children with disabilities.

It did lift my spirits for a while. Something to look forward to. Something normal that other toddlers did. A chance to be with other mothers and babies like us. But she couldn't start until she was 15 months old. It seemed a lifetime away.

My parents tried to encourage Giles and me to spend some time alone together. They offered to have Rachel one evening each week so that we could go out. At first, I was very reluctant, but we gave it a try, and no disasters occurred.

It became a regular thing. It didn't solve all the problems in our marriage, and we ended up talking about Rachel most of the time, but it was a start. We learned to enjoy it, and I know my parents and Rachel enjoyed their time alone together.

I felt guilty for feeling sad. I had Rachel. She was so special. I loved her cute, wonky eyes and her tight little fists that couldn't hold onto anything. I loved her, and she loved me, but it wasn't how it was supposed to be. She wasn't the baby I was meant to have. My baby was supposed to be strong, independent, and active like me.

The 20th of May, 1988, hit me like a bomb. Rachel was one year old! It was a day of mixed emotions. We had a small family party. Rachel was inundated with presents and cards.

The significance of the event was appreciated by everyone. People we hadn't spoken to for months sent gifts and messages of congratulations. Rachel looked more beautiful than ever in her party dress and black patent shoes. I'm not sure which she enjoyed the most - all the fuss and attention, or the birthday cake.

There was an awkward moment when Giles' parents presented her with a baby rocker. My parents had wanted to buy the same toy, but we had been advised against it by LB. We had to be really careful with things like that, as they could increase the limb spasticity that we were working so hard to reduce. Giles and I had already been given a roasting by LB, when we bought Rachel a baby bouncer without consulting her first.

Giles' parents weren't to know, and Giles diplomatically allowed her to play in the rocker for a while, much to my mother's barely concealed distress. But overall, the day went well. Everyone, and especially Rachel, had a great time.

For me, it was both the happiest and saddest day of my life.

Chapter Ten – Picking up the pieces

By the time Rachel was two and a half, we had begun to accept how things were going to be. She had severe developmental delay and was going to need care for the rest of her life. She would never be able to use her hands to pick things up or hold things. She would never be able to walk, and she would never be able to communicate other than by laughing or crying.

But we were beginning to get our lives back together. Rachel was healthy and happy. We had another holiday - this time in Benidorm.

She had the eye surgery that was intended to correct her squint when she was 15 months old. It went well and she recovered quickly. The squint was still there, but it was not as pronounced as it had previously been, unless she was particularly tired.

Soon after that, Rachel started attending the playgroup that LB had mentioned. It was run by the local branch of the Handicapped Children's Association. She loved it, and so did I. It was everything I had hoped it would be. Everyone who worked there was a volunteer and was devoted to the children and families in their care. The service was free and available to anyone who needed it. There were children there with all sorts of disabilities, from cerebral palsy like Rachel, to others with different physical and mental health problems. Rachel attended for a year, from when she was 15 months old until she was nearly two and half.

She made some real connections with some of the other children and developed her own little friendship group. But, equally as important, I made some new friends, too. I met a group of people who genuinely understood our situation – people who really listened when I talked and could offer me invaluable help and advice when I needed it. The other mothers all had their own stories to share, which I could learn from, and the staff were experienced in interacting with countless sets of parents who were going through their own similar, but at the same time, quite different sets of circumstances.

As life settled down, another germ of an idea was forming in my mind. Ever since Rachel had been born, I'd wanted to have another baby. It sounds crazy I know. How could I possibly cope with another baby when I could barely manage with the one I already had? It's hard to explain, and at the time I didn't even fully understand it myself, but I think it was part of my grief for the baby I had lost.

Rachel wasn't the baby I had been expecting. She was someone else. Someone I loved unconditionally and someone who I wanted to be in my life forever, but not the child I had dreamed of during the nine months of my pregnancy, and way before that. That child was gone, and I knew I couldn't have her back, but I still wanted a baby like her – a healthy baby who could do everything that other babies did and would be able to do all the things in the future that I had dreamt of Rachel doing. Was that so wrong?

When I had first broached the idea with Giles, Rachel was still a small baby. He was not at all keen. In fact, he was adamantly against the idea. We were struggling with just the one baby. How on earth would we deal with two? Besides, we were hardly sleeping together. (No, let's be honest, we weren't sleeping together.) We were so focused on Rachel that, when we did get some time alone together, we were both exhausted.

I spoke to some of the other parents at the playgroup about my feelings and they were very encouraging. Some of them had had similar feelings and some had gone on to have other, able-bodied children. But they did ask me if I fully understood what had caused Rachel's cerebral palsy. They suggested I might want to take some medical advice to avoid the same thing happening again.

I spoke to Giles about it again. He was still reluctant, but slightly more open this time. Our lives were getting easier. In a year's time, Rachel would be at school full-time. She was about to start at a local special school for children with additional needs. She would attend part-time until she was three, and could then attend on a full-time basis. It would be just the right time to have another baby.

We took the advice of the other parents and decided to see a genetic counsellor to assess our risk of having another baby with cerebral palsy. The GP referred us without question. Giles and I went together to see Dr. F. in Birmingham, who told us that it was highly unlikely that the same thing would happen again, as what had happened to Rachel had been an accident of birth.

He explained that, during the labour and birth her brain had been starved of oxygen and it was this that had caused the damage. He said that, during the pregnancy and up until the labour, she had almost certainly been a perfectly healthy baby.

I was pleased that we could go ahead and try for another baby, but I was also shocked. No-one had ever put it so clearly to me before. Everyone else had been reluctant to talk about what might, or might not, have caused Rachel's brain damage. Even, Dr, F. didn't really want to discuss it in detail, and refused to put his opinion in writing.

It sowed the seed of an idea with me. The idea that someone else might be to blame for what had happened to Rachel – that it wasn't all my fault after all.

I remembered the trauma of her birth. The concerns Giles and I had expressed again and again about the dips in her heart beat. The hours I had spent frightened and alone on the ward, begging for someone to help me. The way we were left on our own on the labour ward until the morning, when suddenly everything had so quickly gone wrong.

Maybe if someone had taken some notice of what we were saying a bit sooner ...?

Maybe if they hadn't been so busy, and we hadn't been left alone for so long?

Maybe?

Just maybe?

I chatted again to some of the staff and other parents. They were pretty horrified by our story. Most were adamant that what had happened to us wasn't right. A few went a bit further and suggested that we may have been the victims of medical negligence, and that we should consider suing the hospital. One even recommended a solicitor.

I was desperate to find out more about what had happened to Rachel during the birth. I needed to know what had gone wrong. I had to know the truth about what had happened. I needed to know who was responsible, and I needed them to acknowledge, and apologise for, what they had done - or not done, as the case may be. I had carried such an unbearable burden of guilt on my own for so long, I just had to know.

I spoke to Giles about it. He was worried that, even if we did have a case, the cost to undertake something like this would be prohibitive. We didn't know if we could afford it. We thought we might be eligible for legal aid, but we had no idea where to start.

And so, in the spring of 1989, when Rachel was two years old, we decided to approach a solicitor.

We had no experience of dealing with solicitors, other than when we had bought and sold properties, and so, it was our conveyancing solicitors that we first approached. They recommended another local firm who specialised in medical negligence.

We were excited when we set off to see them one morning after dropping Rachel over to my mum's. But our renewed sense of purpose and positivity was quickly deflated when we arrived at the offices. They were situated upstairs through a scruffy off-street doorway on a busy shopping street in a rough area of the city. Things were no better inside. The reception area was shabby and untidy, the solicitor's office dark and dingy, and a musty smell hung in the air. It wasn't a great first impression. It just didn't feel very professional. We were full of doubt.

But the solicitor was lovely: open, warm, and welcoming. He was extremely easy to talk to and came across as very caring and empathetic as we told him our story. He took detailed notes throughout and seemed genuinely appalled by what had happened to us, and to Rachel.

He was sure that we had a case but explained that it would cost around £20,000 for him to take it on. We asked about legal aid, as we knew we couldn't afford this amount, but he told us that our earnings took us over the eligibility threshold. It was disappointing, but we said that we would go away and try to work something out. In the meantime, we did agree to pay him to obtain our medical records. Even if we couldn't afford to fight the case, these documents could at least provide us with the truth about what had happened. Despite the concerns about the finances, it felt good to have finally got the ball rolling.

We had a lot to think about.

Life went on. Rachel left playgroup and started school part-time. It was here that she first met David, a sweet boy who went on to become one of her closest lifelong friends. David took to her straight away. He was a little younger than she was, but he loved to look after her, constantly checking that she was ok, wiping dribble from her chin, talking to her, and playing with her.

Along with the other mothers, at the school, I formed a little, informal support group and, partly ironically, we named ourselves 'The Lucky Mums'. This group also became a huge source of support for me. Rachel continued to see Dr. G. and have her regular physiotherapy and speech therapy, but it was done at playgroup and school instead of at home.

Around this time, she had her first batch of formal medical and educational assessments. The conclusion of her initial medical report was:

"[Rachel] seems to have some language comprehension but virtually no oral expression yet. She is fully dependent on adults for mobility and self-care."

The Educational Psychological Report noted that

she was "cheerful and cooperative" and smiled when spoken to. It also mentioned her excellent hearing and love of music, her "questionable" eyesight, poor language skills and remarkable ability to drink through a straw. All the reports commented on how sociable she was, despite her profound physical disabilities. They all recommended that she needed a highly stimulating learning environment with lots of varied social interaction.

During her life, Rachel went on to have scores of assessments like this. It was so typical of her personality and sense of humour, that she learned to recognise when these were being carried out and was as uncooperative as possible. She would ignore the assessor's requests to perform various tasks or follow their instructions. It amused her to act the fool for them. But she was no fool. If anything, she was making a fool of them. I loved her for that.

LB continued to be absolutely fantastic with Rachel. She had carried on working with her at the playgroup and now at school. Around this time, the neighbour told me about a private physiotherapist called SH, who had been working with her son at home, in addition to his NHS sessions. She was pleased with his progress and suggested we give it a go.

It seemed like a great idea. As Rachel was only at

school five mornings a week, SH could work with her during the time that she was at home. However, I wasn't prepared at all for LB's reaction. She was terribly upset and became very angry with me. I can only imagine that, because she had grown so close to Rachel, she didn't want anyone else intruding on, or interfering with, the work they were doing together. Nevertheless, I decided to go ahead with what I believed would be best for Rachel. Sadly, after that LB never visited us at home again. I will always be grateful for all that she did for Rachel - and for me - during one of the most difficult times of my life.

Another Christmas came and went and, in the New Year I discovered that I was pregnant for the second time. We were so happy. The baby was due in August, around the same time that Rachel started full-time school. It was perfect.

All thoughts of negligence claims and solicitors got put to one side, while I focused on my pregnancy. This time I received my care at a different hospital on the other side of town. I was looked after by a wonderful lady consultant, who was aware of my history. She conducted regular scans and checks on the baby's health and development, and monitored the whole pregnancy and labour like a hawk.

Nevertheless, I was nervous. Towards the end, I had multiple false alarms that had us scuttling back and forth to the hospital every few days. The labour eventually began with what was termed a "heavy show", but to me it was a serious bleed.

I was terrified. But, in the end, Katie, our second daughter, came into the world on the 9th of August, 1990, after a relatively short and easy labour. I'll never forget the moment when she curled her little fingers around mine and I knew she was ok. Rachel had never been able to do that.

We had a challenging first month before Rachel started school full-time. She was jealous of her new sister and demanded more and more of my attention. Mealtimes became a bigger nightmare than ever. I couldn't tend to Katie while I was feeding Rachel. I just had to leave her to cry, and I swear that Rachel took longer than ever to finish her food.

I couldn't take them out together, because I couldn't manage Rachel's chair as well as a pram. Some of the old familiar feelings of isolation and being trapped began to resurface. My days felt more and more chaotic, so it was a relief when Rachel started school full-time and I was able to give Katie more attention during the day.

Even then, the days went by in a blur of getting Rachel ready and taking her to school, caring for Katie and getting the housework done before Rachel was ready to be picked up again. I was still working part-time, too.

When Giles was home, he seemed to be overcompensating for what he perceived to be Rachel receiving less of our attention and spent all his time with her. It was my parents who really got me through this period. They were incredibly helpful and a huge source of encouragement and support.

Over a year had passed since we last saw the solicitor, and we were no closer to working out how we could find the money for the legal fees. But, one day, Giles' dad happened across an article in the paper about legal aid. He cut it out for us. The article explained that, in cases like Rachel's, the victim was often eligible for legal aid, even when their parents were not. It was her case, not ours. We might not be entitled to legal aid, but she could be.

Armed with our newspaper clipping we headed back to the solicitor. We explained to him how we believed we could access legal aid, and he seemed completely unaware of this situation. Nevertheless, he applied for it on our behalf and agreed to proceed with the development of Rachel's case. Looking back, alarm bells about the fact that he didn't fully understand the legal aid process should have been ringing in my head. If Giles' dad hadn't come across the article, we would probably have never taken things any further.

The solicitor told us at this meeting that the hospital had been unable to find any of our medical records. I found this very hard to believe. Rachel was barely three years old. How could all of our medical records have gone missing in such a short period of time? Without them, he had no medical evidence with which to build his case. We were at a standstill.

For me, this aroused a lot of suspicion. I wondered if they were trying to hide something. I started to believe that something untoward had happened that no one had told us about. Rather than dissuading me from carrying on with the legal process, it actually strengthened my resolve to push on.

We soon realised that the legal process is a waiting game of the longest kind. Many months had passed before we went back to see him again. Giles' dad was right. Rachel had no money of her own, so she was entitled to legal aid in her own right. But the medical records had still not been found. We were no further forward.

How could this be? I was even more convinced then, that they had something to hide, and even more determined to find out what had happened.

It was almost a year later that the records finally turned up and we went back to the solicitor for the fourth time. By that time, he had moved to bigger and better premises. He was clearly doing well. He was excited and animated. He was convinced that the reason they had taken so long to turn up was because they had been "altered".

Some things just didn't add up. Their account of events was quite different from my own. The timings, in particular, were way out. He said he was going to write back and challenge them on all the things that didn't seem right.

By the time we left, I was excited, too ... excited and full of hope that, at last, we were getting close to finding out the truth.

So, we were completely devasted when, a few months later, out of the blue, he contacted us and said that he couldn't progress with the case. He said it was bigger and more complex than anything he had ever done before and pretty much admitted that he was out of his depth. He offered to refer us to another firm of solicitors in Coventry, who, in his opinion, would be better placed to help us.

We couldn't believe it. So much time had passed, and we were no further forward. Now we were going to have to start all over again.

Chapter Eleven – Seizures and Solicitors

It was April, 1992 - a month before Rachel's 5th birthday - when we first saw the new solicitor.

By now, Rachel's epilepsy had begun to be an issue for her. She'd had her first admission to hospital with a prolonged and frightening seizure when she was one. At the time, we put it down to a one-off, provoked by changes to her medication, but over time they had become more frequent. She'd had two more admissions when she was two, one when she started school and another just before Christmas. Then, when she was three, she had three more, all around the time she started going to school full-time and when Katie was born.

Her seizures had gradually developed from the tiny finger twitches, that our friend had pointed out to us when she was a baby, into a more distressing form that caused her body to twitch or jerk violently. This could affect just one limb for a few moments, move from limb to limb over a longer period, or affect her entire body for a prolonged period of time. She was always aware of what was happening and would scream throughout, which was very upsetting for everyone, not least her.

However, she also had frequent "absence" seizures each day, when she would just drift off and stare into space for a while. As these did not distress her, we tended to just wait for them to pass and gently bring her back to us by calling her name a few times.

We did have rescue medicine that we could give her when things became bad. In the early days, this consisted of rectal diazepam, which was difficult to administer if she was not at home, and very much hit or miss as to whether it worked or not. In fact, her ability to take her medication properly was part of the problem. Because of her swallowing difficulties, it was impossible to know whether she had actually taken in the correct dose of any of her medications.

Whenever a bout of seizures becomes prolonged, it is called Status Epilepticus. When this occurs, we have no choice but to call an ambulance. It is always a frightening experience, which makes me feel utterly helpless and out of control. But, without exception, the ambulance crews are always amazing. So calm and reassuring.

Most of the time they would categorize Rachel as a "Red" call, and she would be taken straight into Resuscitation and attended to immediately. Occasionally, and often when a more experienced paramedic was involved, they would take a more "relaxed" approach which, ironically, often meant that we would end up having to wait to be seen, with Rachel lying in a distressed state on an uncomfortable trolley, sometimes for several hours.

Her treatment would usually involve heavily sedating her to enable her to "sleep it off", and we were normally able to return home within a day or two. She was always admitted to the Children's Hospital under the care of Dr. G. It was so reassuring whenever he arrived to see her. As soon as he walked into the ward, he would take charge and you knew everything was going to be alright. Everyone clearly respected and admired him, and hung on his every word. We placed our complete trust in him where Rachel's care was concerned, and he never let us down.

As she got older, Rachel's limb spasticity was also becoming more of a problem. Her ankle tendons had shortened and were forcing her feet into a "toe-pointing" position. When we did her standing exercises, she couldn't put her feet flat on the floor. As well as this, her hip muscles were so tight that her legs were constantly being pulled together. It made it difficult for her to do her exercises and for us to handle her easily. SH suggested that she be referred to an orthopaedic consultant to see if there was anything he could do.

Initially, it was proposed that she had surgery to lengthen her ankle tendons, but X-rays revealed that her right hip had dislocated, and it was decided that she needed urgent surgery to correct this.

She had the surgery in 1991, when she was four. During the operation, when her right hip was corrected, the left one immediately dislocated in response. The surgeon decided, without ever discussing it with us, to release the muscles on the inside of both her thighs, in the hope that the tight muscles on the outer thighs would pull everything back into place. It didn't work. For the rest of her life Rachel was left with her legs in what is best described as a "frog-leg" position, making it more difficult than ever to care for her and attend to her daily needs.

Following the operation, she spent six weeks in a plaster cast. Caring for a four-year-old with cerebral palsy who is unable to move her limbs, and still needs to wear a nappy, is a challenge at the best of times. Add a plaster cast into the mix and it becomes near impossible. It was a difficult time for all of us, even for Katie, who at nine months old, needed her share of our time and attention as well.

But Rachel took it all in her stride. Everyone she came into contact with commented on what a delightful, friendly child she was. Her smile captured everyone's heart. She loved to go out for walks and everyone we met would stop to comment on how pretty she was and what a lovely smile she had. She thrived on these interactions. All the people who worked with her loved her from the moment they met her. She hardly ever cried or fussed, whatever the level of pain or discomfort she was in.

But, shortly after the hip surgery, Rachel had another severe seizure that took her back into hospital again.

Looking back, I can now see there was a pattern to her seizures. They almost all occurred at a time when she was experiencing some sort of emotional or physical distress. Now, I wonder whether it was her way of telling us that she was having a hard time.

Life was busy. In 1991, I started to keep a diary. When I look back at the entries, every day was full of physiotherapy sessions, needs assessments, equipment fittings and hospital appointments with various doctors and therapists, many of whom I can't now remember. Mum and Dad baby-sat for us once a week, and Giles and I would go to the cinema or out for a meal. I still met up with The Lucky Mums for coffee from time to time. We had days out and holidays, venturing further afield to Benodet in France.

It was difficult to cope with Rachel's physical needs, as well as look after Katie and carry on working part-time every day. However, work was important to me. It kept me sane. I didn't want to give it up, so I started to employ a home help to give me some additional support. Financially, it was a stretch, but you couldn't put a price on the impact it had on my emotional wellbeing.

Unsurprisingly, time passed and the negligence claim meandered unhurriedly along in the background. But, when we went to see the new solicitor, I was determined to get things moving more quickly.

Our first appointment with them was quite a different experience to our first appointment with the previous solicitor. They were situated in a big, shiny building on a smart business park in Coventry. The contrast between their offices and the scruffy upstairs premises of the previous firm could not have been starker. I was impressed, and full of anticipation that this time things might be different.

I was right. They were professional and efficient.

They had a proven track record with cases like Rachel's. A few months after the first appointment, they had requested a preliminary report from a senior obstetrician in Cambridge, activated our legal aid claim, and received all our files from the old solicitor. They had also written to the hospital requesting new copies of all the medical records. They explained that it was essential to start afresh in the sense that the previous solicitor's approach had "muddied the waters" a little.

They helped us to understand that a claim of this nature was an intricate process, akin to a tense and delicate game of poker. It was important to keep your cards close to your chest and not reveal too much too soon, which could allow your opponents to anticipate your strategy and develop their response in advance. This was where our previous solicitor had got himself into difficulties. Little did we know then that we were going to learn more about this "game" than we could ever had imagined.

The obstetrician's report came through in April, 1993, just before Rachel's 6th birthday. It was long and detailed, but indicated that it was highly likely that medical negligence had occurred. It recommended that an additional report from a neo-natal expert should be obtained. In the meantime, they had sought advice from a barrister about the claim.

This advice did not come back until December, 1993. Again, it was very lengthy and detailed, but highlighted several areas that required further investigation, including the release of the medical records from the health authorities. It also confirmed that the neo-natal report was essential to assess the degree to which poor care might have contributed to Rachel's injuries, and that a further genetic expert opinion should be sought.

During the next few months, the obstetrician produced a second report in response to the barrister's advice. The neo-natal specialist said he could not complete his report without copies of ultrasound scans and X-rays which had still not been provided, and they were struggling to find a suitable expert to provide the genetic opinion. It was not until May, 1994, when Rachel turned seven, that we were informed that the medical notes had finally been found. However, they said they had not retained any hard copies of the scans and X-rays and were unable to provide these.

At this point our solicitors expressed their frustration about working with the health authorities in question and commented on how uncooperative they had been. It was not until December, 1994, that they eventually provided everything that had been requested, and we could finally proceed with the claim and instruct the neo-natal expert to generate his report, which he submitted in January, 1995. At this point, all the relevant reports and records were submitted to the barrister again, to wait his further advice.

We had never imagined the process would be so long and drawn out, but the longer it took, the more determined we were to see it through. In the time it had taken to get to this stage, Rachel had started a new school, had had another admission to hospital with a bowel problem, and two more due to seizures.

The new school had come about when I became increasingly concerned that her old school was not right for her as she got older. In her first year, she had got on really well and struck up a great relationship with her teacher. However, when she moved into her second year, she had a different teacher who didn't seem to understand her as well as the first. The class was bigger, and she was not getting as much one-to-one attention. In addition, most of the children were more able-bodied than her, and she was one of a handful of children who used a wheelchair. Most of the other children had special educational needs, and many had emotional and behavioural problems.

For me, this all served to highlight her disabilities more and seemed detrimental to her development. I started researching other schools in the area that might be better suited to meet her needs. It was when one of the other children had a violent outburst and her wheelchair was damaged, that I decided it was time to take action.

One school in particular, in a less affluent, local authority area, seemed perfect for her. Classes were smaller. Eighty per cent of the children used wheelchairs, and speech therapy and hydrotherapy were integral parts of the curriculum. When I approached our local education authority about this, they were reluctant to consider the transfer. They said they felt that it was better for her to be in a group of children with mixed abilities. They couldn't understand why we would want to transfer her to a school in an area that was more socio-economically deprived than our own.

This was the first time I had challenged the system on what was best for my daughter. I was incensed by the fact that they believed they knew best where she was concerned. I was her mother! I would never do anything that was not in her best interests. Little did I know, this was only the first of a lifetime of battles I was going to have to fight on her behalf.

It quickly became clear to me that the real issue was the cost of the transport she would need to get her over to the school every day. I couldn't believe that they were prepared to put money over Rachel's educational development. How naïve I was back then. But I didn't give up. I made a complete nuisance of myself, challenging every objection they came up with, and contacting them, almost every day, to argue our case.

Eventually, after 12 months of fighting, they conceded, and Rachel started at the new school in September, 1992.

It was perfect for her. She got all the support she needed in a wonderfully caring environment, with a small group of other children like her and staff who understood how to work with families like ours. The hydrotherapy was a fantastic addition to the range of therapies she received. I was encouraged to go along and get into the pool with her when she went swimming a couple of times a week. In the water, she was able to experience a freedom of movement that she couldn't get in any other way. She adored it and I adored sharing these special moments with her.

Ironically, life became even more challenging after she started at the new school. We had to get Rachel up at 6.30am every day to get her washed, dressed and breakfasted before the transport arrived at 8am to take her to school. Getting her ready in time, as well as managing Katie and getting myself ready for work in the morning was exhausting. By now Katie had also developed her own busy little life. It was important to us to ensure that she never missed out on anything because so much of our attention and energy was focused on Rachel. She had sailed through playgroup and had also now started school. We enrolled her in dance classes, which she loved. It filled me with so much joy to watch her dance, but it was always tinged with sadness that Rachel, who loved music so much, would never be able to do the same.

Our evenings were equally as chaotic as our mornings. Rachel had started wearing splints at night to try and reduce her limb spasticity. They were complicated and time consuming to fit. Getting Rachel and Katie ready for bed, and trying to cook and eat dinner and have some time for ourselves was almost impossible. Rachel still didn't sleep well and one or other of us would be up and down all evening to try and settle her, before one of us would go to bed with her around 10pm.

The nights were still hard. Rachel had a very irregular sleep pattern. She would wake frequently and rarely sleep for more than six hours a night, often as little as one. Sometimes, she needed her nappy changed, sometimes her splints were hurting her, and sometimes she just needed to be turned over. It was during this time that we first began to employ carers to help us. At first, we paid for them ourselves. This was before we were able to secure funding from social services for this purpose. It was always a battle to get the right amount of help at the right times from the right people, and we never knew when the funding might be stopped, and the support would dry up.

We started with a few hours each night and gradually built up to having someone every morning for a couple of hours, too. It took a while for us to get used to having other people in our family home. Giles and I had less privacy than ever. But it was worth it. It brought some order to our chaos and gave us the time and energy we needed to try and have a normal family life. Later on, we discovered a wonderful charity that offered support to families like ours. They took over the costs of a carer for 30 hours a week, as well as those of Rachel's physiotherapy sessions with SH, and any specialised equipment she required.

With the additional support from the home help and the carers, and Rachel being at school all day, it felt, for the first time in a long time, like we were beginning to get our own lives back to a certain degree. We were less exhausted, and we even began to develop a social life. We went on more holidays – this time, to Disneyland and Boca Raton in Florida. Rachel had trips away and days out with the school – to Cornwall and to theme parks and the theatre. I also managed to get a few breaks away on my own to visit Louise in Switzerland.

But Giles and I were still very distant from each other. When he was home, he devoted all his energy to Rachel. Our marriage had never really recovered from the initial shock. We went through the motions but the bond between us had gone. I wasn't sure that we would ever get it back.

Apart from the seizures, Rachel's health remained reasonably good. She had never developed any of the recurrent chest infections or the other complications we had been warned about. However, in 1992, she did have her first admission to hospital with dehydration and severe constipation.

Whenever Rachel was unwell or distressed, it immediately affected her will and her ability to eat or drink. She would become very unwell, very quickly, and require hospitalisation so that, during the acute phase, she could be nourished and rehydrated through a naso-gastric tube, and then slowly encouraged to eat and drink again over time.

These were difficult times - uncomfortable and distressing for Rachel, who found the insertion of the naso-gastric tube particularly difficult to tolerate. She would scream and cry, and try to turn her head away as they attempted to insert the tube. But also, terribly worrying and emotionally draining for us to see her suffering and in such a poor state. Like her epilepsy, as she got older, this refusal to eat or drink became more of a problem. As with her epilepsy, I do sometimes wonder if this is her way of communicating with us, consciously or unconsciously, when she is unable to express her feelings in any other way.

Rachel's care and equipment were taking up more and more space. As she got bigger, she became heavier and more difficult to lift and carry. Ideally, she needed a ground floor bedroom with access to a bathroom. We applied to the council for a grant to enable us to convert our garage into a ground floor bedroom and bathroom for her.

Yet again, nobody seemed to want to help us. Yet again, I had to fight to get Rachel what she needed.

After months of debate and discussion, they finally agreed to give us some of the money, and we were able to proceed with the work. Having the extra space made a huge difference to our lives, and caring for Rachel became so much easier. Even Giles and I started getting along a little better. In fact, towards the end of 1994, when the work was nearing completion, we started talking about having another baby. We both felt it would be good for Katie to have a little brother or sister to play with.

Once we made our minds up, it wasn't long before I was pregnant again. Rachel was seven and Katie was five. We were delighted.

This time I was much less fearful about what might happen and able to really enjoy the pregnancy, and look forward to having a new baby. But it was hard being pregnant and caring for a disabled seven-year-old and an active five-year-old. Towards the end, lifting Rachel became particularly difficult. But again, as with Katie, the ante-natal care I received was outstanding. Even when I was induced 10 days early because of a potential problem with the baby, I never had any doubt that I was in safe hands.

Brooke was born, strong and healthy on the 7th of July, 1995. It was a wonderful time. We were all so much more relaxed and able to enjoy her arrival. Katie adored her new little sister and even Rachel seemed to be less troubled by the latest addition to the family.

Don't get me wrong, it was harder work than ever. Brooke was not an easy baby. She was always hungry, and she was a crier. Not as bad as Rachel had been, but a crier, nonetheless. She also had a bad bout of gastroenteritis when she was just six weeks old, requiring an admission to hospital and creating all sorts of problems in terms of caring for her sisters.

It was hard work, but we were happy. Happy to have another beautiful daughter. Happy to have created a loving, little family with Rachel at its heart.

Not long after Brooke was born, we finally heard back from the barrister. They were ready to take the case to the next stage. A meeting was arranged in London on the 7th of December between us, the barrister, our solicitor, and the obstetric and neo-natal experts.

Chapter Twelve – Scans and Scoliosis

The conference in December was the first of many similar meetings that took place in the barrister's chambers in London. Typically, they involved our legal team, several medical experts, and us, all sitting around a table.

Giles and I were a young, working couple from Birmingham. We found ourselves suddenly immersed in a world that we hadn't known existed: a bewildering and daunting world of opulent rooms in grand buildings that lined leafy squares in parts of the capital that oozed wealth and privilege.

We were excited and intimidated at the same time. At the first couple of meetings, we only spoke when we were asked to, and that wasn't very often. Sometimes it felt as though we were invisible. Loud and pompous, middle-aged, middle-class men discussed our lives and our family as though we weren't there. They had no idea what our lives were like, and it honestly felt as though they didn't care. I found it hard to believe that they had Rachel's best interests at heart. The only interests they seemed to be concerned about were their own.

On one occasion, over a discussion about the number of tumble driers we got through, our barrister asked why we hadn't bought a better quality machine at the outset: one that would last longer than the cheap ones we were buying - like a Miele for example. On another occasion, one of the medical experts was asked to leave the room by our barrister after referring to Rachel's brain as being like a piece of Emmental cheese.

Nevertheless, these conferences were an essential and important part of the legal process, and they always moved things forward, albeit very slowly. After the first one, it was agreed that Rachel needed to have an up-to-date MRI scan of her brain. The first neo-natal specialist who had prepared a report was unable to arrange this, so another expert had to be found who was willing and able to do so. In February, 1996, someone was identified, but in May, they explained that they could not do the scan themselves but could recommend someone else who could.

Every single step of the process took months to achieve. In addition, every activity that incurred a fee had to be approved by the Legal Aid Board before it could take place. Almost every time, this approval was denied and questioned in the first instance, necessitating an appeal before it was approved, and we could go ahead.

In the end, the scan did not take place until the 17th of April, 1997 - almost 18 months after it had been requested. This was due in part to all the legal wrangling between the experts, the legal team and the Legal Aid Board, as well as cancellations due to staff shortages ... but also to a degree of anxiety on my part.

For Rachel to have the scan, she would need to be sedated, because she would not be able to keep still for the procedure. Every intervention like this carries a degree of risk, and for Rachel this risk is higher than for the average person. I was unhappy about putting her through this, simply to provide evidence for the legal case. It just seemed highly unnecessary and unethical to me.

As it happened, though, around the same time, Rachel had developed a painful swelling at the base of her spine. Dr. G. suspected that this may be the source of frequent unexplained episodes of fever and the increased number of seizures she was having. He felt that an MRI scan may be useful in terms of helping him understand what was going on. In this way, with a bit of liaison and cooperation between the different medical teams, the scan went ahead for both medical and legal purposes.

Once the results of the scan had been analysed, another expert medical report was produced. A couple of doctors were involved in compiling this to the satisfaction of our solicitor. These reports were circulated and discussed, and yet more reports sought and produced from a never-ending stream of experts. Some obliged; some didn't. Some requested additional information; some asked to see Rachel in person. Some felt we had a case and some didn't - and every step had to cross the hurdle of Legal Aid approval.

Over time, the solicitors in the partnership came and went. I think we had gone through at least two or three before the final one, JW, took over Rachel's case in May, 1996. She ended up being the person who saw it through to the very end. She was hard-working, patient and persistent. I trusted her to get the job done. She was always practical, logical and efficient, and never emotional. She never met Rachel in person, and I suspect this was a deliberate strategy on her part to enable her to maintain that professional detachment.

By April, 1998, when Rachel was approaching her 11th birthday, we had reached another hiatus. We had a plethora of reports and opinions, from a plethora of experts, but none of them seemed to be able to agree on one thing. They *could* agree that Rachel had received a serious injury to her brain around the time of her birth but could not be more specific about whether this occurred before or during the labour, and whether it was due to medical negligence or not. It was decided that it was necessary to hold another conference with all the medical experts together in one room, to try and resolve this once and for all.

The conference was set for the 29th of July, 1998.

In the midst of all of this, Rachel was fighting another, more serious battle of her own. Just after Christmas in 1997, the school asked me to come in to see the orthopaedic consultant, who was attached to the school. I arrived early and, as there was no one on reception, made my way straight into the room where the clinics were usually held. I couldn't help but notice some x-rays that had been left on the viewing box. The images were of a child's spine. It was horribly deformed, curved into a big "C" shape at the base. I was shocked and wondered who it belonged to, feeling for the poor child and their parents, whoever they may be.

As I sat there, it began to dawn on me, that they might be Rachel's x-rays. No-one had come out of the room before I went in, or was waiting to be seen. Rachel had been troubled by the ongoing problem of a painful swelling at the base of her spine, and she'd had various scans and x-rays to investigate this, but no-one had ever discussed the results with us. I had just assumed that they were all fine.

My heart began to pound in my chest. By the time the doctor came into the room, I was distraught.

"Please tell me that's not Rachel's spine?" I pleaded with him.

"I'm afraid it is," he replied.

He went on to explain that Rachel had developed severe scoliosis. It is a common problem in children with cerebral palsy. As the spine grows and develops, it can be pulled out of position by the muscle spasticity. In Rachel's case, it had become very severe ... so severe, that it was beginning to compress her lungs and other vital organs, and her life was now in danger. She was at extremely high risk of developing recurrent, life threatening respiratory infections and other complications. The only thing that could save her was major surgery to correct the curvature by breaking and straightening the spine, removing and replacing some of her ribs with coral, and inserting metal rods into her back to keep it all in place.

I was devastated. One of the teachers was waiting outside for me and I fell into her arms, sobbing. She told me that the school had known about the problem for a few weeks but had made the decision not to tell us until after Christmas, to enable us to enjoy our family time together over the holidays.

It was shocking how quickly Rachel deteriorated. She was seen very quickly by a surgeon and put on the waiting list at a specialist orthopaedic hospital, but there was a nine-month waiting list for procedures like hers.

She became sicker and sicker. She had one chest infection after another. Her breathing was laboured all the time. She was losing her sparkle. I could see her fading away in front of my eyes. I began to fear that she would not survive long enough to get her operation.

My friend, Louise, was horrified that this could be allowed to happen ... that a child could wait so long for a life-saving operation that she could die before the surgery was performed. In an act of incredible generosity, she phoned me one day to tell me that she wanted to pay for Rachel to have the surgery performed privately.

I'll be honest, I didn't argue with her. We were being thrown a lifeline and we grabbed it with both hands.

Rachel had her surgery on the 9th of June, 1998 - three weeks after her 11th birthday. The surgery was performed by the same surgeon, at the same hospital it would have been done, had she had it done on the NHS, but almost six months earlier. I knew she would never have survived that long, and that I was so fortunate to have a friend like Louise who could help us in this way.

Not everyone saw it that way, though. I definitely got the feeling that there were some people who thought this was "nature's way" of ending Rachel's "suffering". One mother at Brooke's playgroup actually told me that, face to face. She accosted me in the kitchen area where we waited to collect our toddlers and told me, in front of all the other mothers, that I was being cruel and selfish to put Rachel through the operation - that it was time to just let her die in peace.

I was literally speechless. I couldn't believe it! Thankfully, a close friend who knew Rachel, and knew how much she enjoyed life, jumped to my defence. Some of the other mothers, who were horrified by the woman's comments, joined in. I was incredibly grateful for their support, but it was still a terribly upsetting incident.

Was that how people saw me? Someone who would put their own daughter through unnecessary pain and suffering to prolong what they saw as a miserable life. I was shattered.

Rachel was admitted the day before the surgery for tests and a full anaesthetic assessment. She had her own room, which meant I could stay with her. But I barely slept. It was going to be a lengthy and difficult procedure, one not without risks.

The words of the woman at the school echoed in my head. Was it right to put her through this? What if it went wrong and she was worse off than before? What if she died during the operation? But what choice did we have? Rachel loved life. Every day of our lives was filled with her smiles and laughter. There was no choice. We had to do it!

We took her down at 8am the following morning. I was shocked to see how many people were arriving to take part in the operation. It was clearly a big deal for them, too. They all had drinks and lunchboxes with them. It was expected to take between 10 and 12 hours. They were going to be in there all day.

I wept as they wheeled her away. What if this turned out to be the last time I saw her? What if I never saw her beautiful smile again?

The nursing staff encouraged us to go home. They thought it would be easier than sitting in her empty room all day. We took their advice, but it wasn't easier at all. We felt so far away. We couldn't settle. We tried to eat, but we weren't hungry. We tried to watch TV but ended up just flicking through the channels before turning it off. We were tired, so we tried to lie down for a while. But we couldn't sleep. What if something went wrong? It would take us ages to get back to the hospital. What if she needed us?

We stuck it out till the afternoon but were back in her empty room by 4pm. The time crawled by. At 6pm, 10 hours in, we were hoping and expecting some news but there was nothing. It was ok, we told ourselves. They said it could take 12 hours. But by 8pm, there was still no news. I was frantic ... pacing the floor ... watching the corridor for anyone approaching.

Around 9pm, I saw Rachel's anesthetist walking up the corridor towards us. I braced myself for what was coming ... fearing the worst. But he walked right past our door.

That was it! I knew something was wrong. I knew he was preparing to tell us that she had passed away.

I burst out of the room and ran after him.

"Please tell me! Tell me what's happened. I know you're hiding something from us!"

He was astonished.

"No, I'm not. She's fine. She's still in surgery. Another anesthetist is looking after her while I take a break."

It had never entered my head that they were working in shifts. Of course, they were. They had to take breaks and cover each other.

I felt so stupid. I went back to the room. But at least I knew she was still alive.

It was around 10pm when they finally told us she was in recovery, and 11pm by the time we were allowed to see her in HDU. She was awake and as soon as she saw us her face lit up in a smile. I had never been so happy to see Rachel's magical smile. She had done it. She had survived. Again!

Her surgeon came to see us. He was so excited to tell us the good news, that he had not even changed his clothes. He was covered in Rachel's blood. Giles was so shocked that he almost passed out and had to go outside for some air. But he soon recovered when he heard the news.

The operation had been a great success. He showed us the x-rays. He had reduced the curvature in Rachel's spine to zero! Not only had she survived the surgery, but she was going to be absolutely fine!

Like the little fighter that she is, she made an amazingly quick recovery. She was back home, laughing and smiling and running us all in circles after just 10 days.

Also, during this time, we had begun to explore the idea of respite care. Life was hectic, caring for Rachel, Katie, and Brooke and both of us working - me part-time and Giles full-time. Sometimes, I worried that the two younger girls were missing out on things because of the way our family was centred around Rachel's care. Giles and I were still exhausted all the time. If we could find somewhere that could look after Rachel for a few hours now and again, it would enable us to spend some quality time with the other two girls and give us the chance to rest and recharge our batteries.

I knew we were eligible for respite but finding somewhere suitable that would accept her became yet another battle that we had to fight.

I did all the usual research to find out what was available. I found a local branch of a well-known national organisation that had a good reputation and booked Rachel in for an assessment. But they refused to take her, saying that she was too severely disabled to qualify. It just didn't make any sense. Surely, we were in more need than families who had "less" disabled children? I was disgusted.

The next option was a local centre, which specialised in respite care for disabled children. This time they accepted her, and she started going for a few hours on odd occasions. But I never felt comfortable about the place. It was two old police houses that had been knocked into one. It was grey and dingy and always smelt dank and unpleasant. The staff seemed kind and caring, but there were so few of them. They couldn't possibly give all of the children the full care they required. I couldn't relax and enjoy my free time as I felt guilty about leaving her there.

One day, when I went to pick her up, I saw her

through the window - my beautiful, friendly, sociable Rachel, sitting alone in her wheelchair, facing the wall. It broke my heart. I never took her back.

In January, 1997, the same children's charity that had helped us in the past with homecare and equipment, offered to fund a respite place for Rachel in a facility in Hereford. It was a wonderful place, a modern, purpose-built, 12-bedded, residential centre for children and adults with profound disabilities, set in beautiful grounds. It had everything she could possibly need, including high quality nursing care, a hydrotherapy pool, a sensory room and group, speech and language therapy. It was perfect.

Rachel started going there for one weekend a month. It was a long drive - a three-hour round trip on a Friday and again on the Sunday - but it was worth it.

Rachel loved it and we loved it. We were able to relax and enjoy our free time in the knowledge that she was happy and well cared for.

With everything else that had been going on, the big medical experts conference came sooner than we expected.

Just six weeks after Rachel's surgery, we settled

her into respite for a couple of days and went home to get ready for our trip to London.

Chapter Thirteen – Dramas and Disasters

The phone rang when we were in the middle of trying to settle the girls down for the night. They were excited about spending the day with my parents while we were away in London.

It was JW. She had bad news. The meeting was going to have to be postponed. One of the key experts had a family emergency. His two children had been involved in an accident and were both in different hospitals. There was no way he could make it.

We were disappointed. It was a big blow. It had taken so long to find a date when everyone could attend. Who knew how long it would be before it could be rescheduled?

I decided to look on the bright side and make the most of our unexpected free day with the girls and my parents. We decided to have a day out together – well, all that is except for Giles, who chose not to join us, instead taking the opportunity to have a quiet day to himself.

The rest of us had a wonderful day at Legoland. It was after 10pm by the time we got back, and I was surprised to find that Giles was not at home. It was before the days of mobile phones, and there was no note, but I assumed he'd gone to the pub. He sometimes went for a drink with my brother. I settled the girls down and got into bed myself.

By 11pm he still wasn't back. I was a little worried but assumed that he was on his way.

I must have dozed off, as I woke a few hours later to find the bed still empty beside me. Now, I was very concerned! Where was he? Something must have happened to him. I didn't know what to do. It was the middle of the night. I couldn't call anyone. I couldn't leave the girls to go and look for him. Besides, where would I go?

When he still wasn't home by 5am, I was frantic. I called my parents, who woke my brother. Den confirmed that he had been at the pub with Giles, but that they'd left well before closing time. I rang round all the local hospitals. One had someone fitting his description in A&E. They said he was drunk and sleeping it off and I shouldn't hurry in.

I was horrified. It just wasn't like him. He'd never

done anything like this before.

I asked my mum to come over and watch the girls, and I was at the hospital by 6am. Giles was on his own in a cubicle with the curtains closed. He was completely unresponsive. He was still in his clothes from the night before. They were dirty and torn. There was dried blood around his nostrils. No one seemed to know what had happened to him, just that he had been brought in by ambulance the previous evening around 11pm. I couldn't understand why I couldn't wake him up. He never drank that much. Something wasn't right.

Everyone was too busy to talk to me. It took an hour before I managed to speak to the doctor and he told me that Giles did have a head injury, a fractured skull in fact, but the main problem was that he he'd had too much to drink, and they couldn't assess him properly until the alcohol was out of his system. I explained that this was completely out of character. The doctor reluctantly examined him again but didn't change his opinion.

By 9am, I still couldn't rouse him. Despite what the medical and nursing staff were saying, I was really concerned. I called his brother and, as he was at work, he sent Giles' sister-in-law in to sit with us. At 11am, we were so worried that we decided to call his parents, who were on holiday in

Bournemouth, and suggested they should come home. He was still completely unresponsive. People came in and out and checked on him, but no one seemed particularly concerned. It was 4pm before we finally persuaded them to take his condition seriously. They took him for a scan.

After that, everyone suddenly started rushing around. It turned out that Giles wasn't drunk and "sleeping it off". The scan had shown that he had a serious head injury. A large blood clot was pressing on his brain. He needed urgent surgery to remove it and save his life. He wasn't just sleeping. He was in a coma.

Within minutes, we were in an ambulance speeding across the city to another hospital. He was whisked into surgery the moment we arrived. He was in the operating theatre until around midnight, when he was transferred to Intensive Care. His surgeon told us that he had removed the clot but that he was still in a coma. He said that we would have to wait and see whether he woke up or not, and, if he did, whether he would have any lasting brain damage.

I couldn't take it in. I couldn't believe this was happening to us after everything else we had been through. It didn't feel real.

Mum and Dad looked after the girls, and Rachel remained in respite, while we waited to see if Giles would recover.

He was in a coma for 10 days. When he woke up, he had no idea where he was or what had happened to him. He also had a broken collar bone and various cuts and bruises. I gently asked him what he remembered about his life. When I showed him pictures of the girls, he remembered Rachel and Katie, but had no idea who Brooke was, saying, "I don't know who she is, but she's very pretty, isn't she?"

He knew I was his wife, but he couldn't remember my name. He poured custard on his dinner and gravy on his pudding and ate it all regardless. When he watched TV, he thought he was in another country, as he thought the characters were speaking in a foreign language.

A police investigation was initiated, and we began to find out bits and pieces about what had happened to him. My brother said he had left the pub around 9pm. He'd borrowed his dad's fold-up bike to cycle home across the park. He was found around 11pm, lying in the road by a couple of girls who had just finished work at a nearby fish and chip shop, and it was them who had called the ambulance. There had been no sign of his bike at the scene, but the police found it a few days later in the back garden of a house in the vicinity. The old man who had "found" it, had cleaned it up and was planning to sell it.

It appeared that, because his clothes were dirty and torn and he'd had a couple of drinks, the general assumption had been that he was a drunk vagrant, who just needed to be left alone to "sleep it off". If they had only taken the time to check his pockets, they would have found his wallet, like I did the following morning. It contained his money, credit cards and pictures of his family, and would immediately have shown them that he was a normal working man with a family at home who would be wondering where he was. It also contained his address and telephone number, which they could have used to contact us to let us know where he was. It's awful, but maybe if they had not assumed that he was just another drunk vagrant, they would have paid him more attention and prevented at least some of the brain damage he will have to live with for the rest of his life.

We never did find out exactly what had happened to Giles that night. The police investigation was eventually closed, and as Giles himself has no memory of the incident, it will always remain a mystery.

But everything changed from that moment on for us. Our lives went into freefall. While he was in hospital, my parents continued to look after Katie and Brooke. Our entire extended family was under severe stress. Louise even flew over to help out.

The ward he was on was a disturbing place, full of people like him and worse. I didn't want the girls to visit him there. I was worried about the impact it could have on them to see so many people in such distressing conditions. Eventually, Louise, as generous as ever, paid for him to be transferred to a private hospital, where he had his own room and the girls could visit. Rachel remained in respite. They looked after her for as long as we needed them to. They were a lifeline for us during this time. I don't know how we would have coped without them.

The first six months of his recovery were the most intense, but he needed months of rehabilitation after that. At first, he slept a lot of the time. He had to learn to walk and talk all over again. After a while, he began to spend short periods at home, gradually building up towards his discharge.

When he was at home, he followed me around the house like another child, but a child that thought he was an adult. He didn't realise that he couldn't do the things he used to do. He thought there was nothing wrong with him. If I hung out the washing, he would re-hang it all. If I loaded the dishwasher, he would take it all out and do it all over again. He wasn't safe to drive or look after the girls, but he thought he was. He couldn't go back to work, but he couldn't understand why. All his old personality traits, good and bad, were exaggerated. He was emotionally volatile and quick to anger. We began to have frequent arguments.

I knew I had to try to be patient and caring, but it was extremely difficult. I was at my wits' end, exhausted, frustrated, angry and upset, all at the same time. Not only was I dealing with looking after Rachel and the girls, and running our home on my own, but now I had him to care for as well. It was around this time that Rachel began to spend alternate weeks in respite, just to give me a bit of a break.

But, six weeks after Giles' accident, *my* body decided it had had enough and I was admitted to hospital myself.

Back when we'd been in the ambulance, racing across the city to save Giles' life, I had developed a pain in my chest. It was like a knife, stabbing through me. I couldn't breathe. I was sure I was having a heart attack. I thought *I* might be dying as well.

I was sitting in the front next to the driver, as the

other paramedic and a nurse worked on Giles in the back. I didn't want to say anything, but it became so bad that I had to.

"I'm so sorry to do this to you, but I think I'm having a heart attack."

The paramedic looked at me. I couldn't work out his facial expression. I knew how crazy I sounded.

"Honestly! I have a terrible pain in my chest."

"I'm sorry, but you'll just have to hold on till we get there. We can't deal with that at the moment. We must get Giles to the hospital. When we get there, we'll get them to have a look at you."

But, by the time we got there, the pain had gone.

Six weeks later, it returned. It hit me totally out of the blue. We were in a church at a christening. I'd had to drive us all there after getting everyone ready. The pain was sharp and stabbing like before … like a knife plunging deep inside me. I couldn't breathe.

I went outside for some air, but it got worse. Somehow, I managed to get everyone home before I collapsed in agony. I asked Giles to call an ambulance, but he couldn't do it. He looked at the phone but couldn't work out what to do. Instead, he was able to call my mother who called the ambulance for me.

At the hospital, they suspected I had a blood clot on my lung and started me on anticoagulant treatment. I was in hospital for 10 days. In the end, the clot didn't show up on any tests, but they said it could be because the treatment had dispersed it before I had the scans. Looking back, I believe this was the start of my own problems with stress and anxiety – a result of everything I had gone through.

It was months before we were able to pick up where we left off with the legal case. When we did, we were hit by yet another blow. The whole case was based on our account of what had happened during the labour, and Giles was a key witness to this. Now, because of his head injury, he was no longer fit to take the stand and, because of his own brain damage, was no longer regarded as a credible witness.

It was now only my word against theirs. We were right back to square one.

Chapter Fourteen – Progress and PTSD

Even after everything that had happened in the past, the next couple of years were the most unhappy of my entire life. I was miserable, exhausted, and lonely. Giles' condition improved over the first six months, but then he reached a plateau. He was still confused, had severe memory loss and was uninhibited and unpredictable. He went back to work after a year, but in a different job. He didn't understand that he couldn't do the job he had done before, and this was another great source of frustration for him.

He was a completely different person. It was as if another man was occupying his body. Even his physical mannerisms had changed. I felt as though I was living with a complete stranger. I didn't know him anymore. I still loved and cared for him, but like a particularly good friend or a sister, not as a wife. Any last vestiges of our marriage had finally shrivelled and died.

But I soldiered on, caring for him and all the girls. I was on automatic pilot – never questioning what I had to do, just getting on with doing it … getting on with what had become my life.

Giles and I began to live separate lives. At first, we did try to go out together from time to time and even have a few family holidays, but I never knew when he was going to do, or say, something inappropriate or embarrassing. I was on edge all the time and never able to relax around him. Eventually, it became impossible, and we did less and less together as a couple. I began to build a social life of my own, outside of the home, going out on my own with friends whenever I got the rare opportunity to do so.

There was one memorable occasion, when we had decided to have a short family holiday in Tenerife with the two younger girls. Rachel was booked into respite for the week. We tried to do things like this without her from time to time. It was important for us all to have regular breaks from her care, to rest and recharge and to focus all our attention on the other two girls. We had only been there a few hours, when we got a call from the respite facility to say that Rachel had been admitted to hospital with a suspected blood clot in her leg. I was frantic. I had to get home to her. But I couldn't leave Giles on his own with the girls. He wouldn't have been able to cope. So, we all had to go. There was no choice.

I spent hours working out how we could all get home. We ended up having to fly business class to Madrid and then from Madrid to Heathrow. Our car was at Gatwick, so we had to get a taxi to collect it, then drive all the way back up to Hereford. Giles still couldn't drive, so I had to do all of the driving myself. By the time we made it to her bedside, we were all completely frazzled and exhausted.

Rachel, on the other hand, was absolutely fine. She roared with laughter when she saw our anxious faces. The whole chain of events had begun when one of the staff had noticed that her right foot was colder than her left and was concerned that a blood clot might be blocking her circulation. She didn't know that Rachel's foot was always cold. It was a complication of her scoliosis surgery. For some reason, the hospital was also treating her for asthma, which she has never had, neither before nor since.

So, after all that we had put ourselves through, it turned out that there was actually nothing wrong with her.

Eighteen months after Giles' accident, a good

friend took me to one side and told me that he was really worried about me. He said he'd never seen me so low, and he was right. He asked me to think carefully about my life and what I wanted. He told me that I wasn't responsible for what had happened to Giles and that I didn't have to stay with him just because I believed it was the right thing to do. He said I didn't have to stay in a loveless marriage just because my husband had suffered a brain injury, and that I had enough to deal with caring for Rachel and the girls. I didn't have to look after Giles as well. There were other people who could do that.

It was just what I needed to hear. There was a way out of the miserable situation that my life had become. That evening I sat Giles down after the girls were in bed and told him that I couldn't continue living the way we were, and that I wanted a divorce. I felt terrible, riddled with guilt about seeming to abandon him when he needed me most, but in my heart, I knew I was doing the right thing for both of us. There was nothing left of our marriage. He had never once told me he loved me since his accident. As far as we were both concerned, I was simply his carer! I just couldn't do it anymore.

He was devastated … utterly distraught. He fetched a bucket from the kitchen and started retching into it as I talked. I think it was just the shock. I honestly believe he, too, knew that it was the right decision. He never once asked me to change my mind or made suggestions about how we could "work it out". I think it was an inevitable climax that he knew was coming, but at the same time, he hoped it would go away if he didn't acknowledge it.

Understandably, he didn't want to leave the family home. He loved his daughters and didn't want to live away from them, and he was still battling with his recovery after his accident. But that was the only way it could work. I couldn't leave him. I couldn't remove Rachel from the house that was adapted to meet her needs, where all her equipment was, and all her care was delivered. It was impossible.

A breakdown in any long-term relationship is always a difficult and complex process. It becomes even more so when children are involved. When one of those children is severely disabled, and one of the parties has suffered a serious brain injury, it becomes a living hell.

It took 12 months before Giles finally left the family home. He clearly didn't want to go and did everything he could to avoid the move. He said he wouldn't leave unless he could have 50% of the equity from the house, equal access to all the children, and not pay any maintenance. I had to do everything. I had to sort out the finances, the solicitors and even find him somewhere to live. I had to re-mortgage the house, based on my part-time salary and work out some complex childcare arrangements. He did nothing. I think he thought that if he just sat it out, I would give up, and we would continue as we were.

During the year before he left, we lived totally separate lives in the same house. We didn't sleep together anyway, because one of us always slept with Rachel, but now we went out separately and, when we were at home, spent little time in the same room together.

It was a difficult time. But I didn't give up. I kept plodding on, sorting out one challenge after another until, eventually, the day came when he moved out and into his own flat. It was a huge release for me. I couldn't believe it had finally happened. But it left me drained, emotionally and physically. The new childcare arrangements worried me. I couldn't see how they were going to work, but I had to try. I had to make them work for all our sakes.

Giles' flat was on the ground floor and adapted to meet Rachel's needs. The plan was that the children would spend one week with him and one week with me. On the weeks they were with him, I would go over and help him get them all ready for school in the mornings, as well as pick them up from school, give them dinner and look after them until he got home from work. My life looked as though it was going to be even more hectic than ever.

I was right. The arrangements didn't suit anyone, and only lasted a few weeks. Giles admitted that he couldn't cope with Rachel and only wanted Katie and Brooke to stay with him. Katie wasn't happy about this and said, if Rachel wasn't going to be there, she didn't want to be there either. She didn't like being at Giles' for whole weeks at a time, and this would be even worse if Rachel wasn't going to be there. She wanted to live at home and just visit him when she wanted. It was at this point that I decided to get social services involved. I couldn't make these sensitive and difficult decisions on my own. Neither of us could. We were too embroiled in the complex emotions of it all. After reviewing our circumstances, Social Services recommended that the children should all live with me and just see Giles for regular, but shorter visits. It was such a relief.

As well as feeling generally very down, it was around this time that I started having flashbacks and panic attacks. I'd find myself reliving things that had happened in the past, like Rachel's birth and Giles' accident. They would replay in my mind over and over again, almost in slow motion. I would examine every tiny detail, questioning whether I could have done anything differently, anything that could have prevented or changed the outcomes. I'd recall other things too, all in vivid detail: trips to the hospital in the back of an ambulance with Rachel; the other babies and children in Special Care and on the children's wards; other patients on the neurology ward where Giles had been treated; patients I had seen in accident and emergency departments, all suffering, in pain or dying.

These memories would make me feel so powerless and unable to help or change anything, that I would become stressed and anxious. My heart rate would speed up and I would feel as if I couldn't breathe. I'd feel dizzy and sick. Sometimes I could cry, sometimes I couldn't. I would be trapped in a waking nightmare. Sometimes I would scream out loud. Sometimes all I could do was scream inside my head. No-one could help me with these attacks. I would become distant and irritable. There was no escape, no release. They could last for days with no respite. I couldn't eat or sleep. They would leave me utterly depleted and exhausted.

But I recognised them for what they were and took myself along to the GP. She said she was surprised I hadn't had problems like this sooner, and prescribed me some diazepam and referred me for counselling. I didn't get on with the diazepam. It made me sleepy and lethargic, and my life was too busy for me to feel like that. Too many people needed me, depended on me. I didn't hit it off with the first counsellor either, and only went along for a couple of sessions. But at least I had acknowledged that I had a problem and had made a start in terms of dealing with the impact on my mental health of everything I had gone through.

Since then, I have had two prolonged periods of counselling, both of which lasted around two years. I have been diagnosed with PTSD. I have learned to recognise what my triggers are and have developed my own techniques to manage my condition. For example, I have a tendency to "ambulance chase". Whenever I hear a siren or see an ambulance, I am immediately transported into the back of the ambulance, being rushed to hospital with Rachel in a critical state. I am now able to recognise when this happens and stop myself from being drawn into it. I don't need medication, and I have not required any counselling for many years. Nevertheless, whenever I am under stress or pressure, I feel some of my symptoms threatening to return and I have to take myself out of whatever situation it is that is causing the problem.

I am also learning to cope with the constant fear that my daughter might suddenly become seriously ill and die. I have lived with this fear from the day she was born. It is crippling. Every night, for 33 years, I have gone to bed not knowing whether she will still be here in the morning. Over the years, we have attended the funerals of so many of her friends and peers, always grateful that she is still with us, but always knowing that it could just as easily be her. Whenever she is ill, this fear intensifies. I wonder if this will be her time. I whisper to her, telling her how much she is loved and encouraging her to fight. She always does. Somehow, she always pulls through. It never ceases to amaze me how strong and resilient she is. But I should know that; she proved that on the day she was born. I take great comfort from it.

I also draw comfort from my strong faith in spirit. Whilst I lost my faith in God many years ago, I have developed a strong belief that the spirit survives after death and that there is more to the world and our lives here, and in the hereafter, than we will ever know. I have become a spiritual medium in order to share my faith with others and use it to help and support them with their personal issues and challenges. What this means for me is that I have a strong belief that, when you have served your purpose on earth and it is time for you to pass, nothing will change that. When Rachel's time comes, I will take comfort in that. That said, I cannot begin to imagine what my life will be like without her in it. It is as if she is part of me. As if we are one person. I have been her mother, her friend, her advocate, and her voice for 33 years. I cannot imagine it being any other way.

It was also around this time that I first met Steve. He was working as a doorman at a local bar - one of my favourite haunts whenever I could wangle a night out with my friends. He had already caught my eye - a big, burly, bear of a man with a twinkle in his eye and a wicked sense of humour. One night, as I was leaving, he asked for my phone number and I gave it to him without a moment's hesitation.

I wasn't ready for another serious relationship, but then again, neither was he. He'd split from his first wife recently too, and we were both still very raw. So, at first, we just remained friends. Very good friends, but just friends all the same. He became a huge source of support to me. You couldn't meet a more kind and caring man. He was the complete antithesis of his intimidating physical persona.

Even more importantly, Rachel adored him from the day she met him, and he her. They settled in to each other as if they had known one another for years. There was no awkwardness on his part. Some people are uncomfortable around Rachel. They don't seem to know what to do or say, and how to behave. Steve was never like that. He treated her the same as he treated everyone else: with irreverence, wit, and wisdom. Equally, Rachel knows who she likes and who she does not. She has an uncanny ability to see through people. To sort out the wheat from the chaff. She may not be able to talk or communicate in any of the usual ways, but if she doesn't like someone, they will know it. Believe me!

We continued like this for about a year before

our friendship blossomed into a romance. When it did, it was the proverbial whirlwind. We fell madly in love very quickly and have been inseparable ever since.

In spite of all the drama and upheaval in our family life, Rachel's was thriving during this period. She had recovered well from her surgery. She loved school, had developed a busy social life and was generally happy and content. Apart from a couple of admissions with epilepsy, and a couple of episodes of refusing to eat with resultant dehydration, her health was good too. I had the inevitable stream of wrangles with the local authorities over various aspects of her care, this time including changes to her night cover and the removal of funding for her night splints. It was all as frustrating and draining as ever for me, but, for Rachel, overall, it was a relatively stable period as far as her care was concerned.

In the background to all of this, the legal battle rumbled on. After the July conference was cancelled, the key neo-natal neurology expert pulled out, stating that he believed there was no chance of a successful claim in Rachel's case. He was of the opinion that it was not possible to definitively tell exactly when the injury to Rachel's brain had occurred. This meant that the opinion of yet *another* expert had to be sought, and yet *another* report produced, that would be customarily first rejected and subsequently approved by Legal Aid.

It was not until January, 2000, almost 18 months later, that this report was finally complete, and we moved into the next stage of the process.

This involved sending a Pre-issue Protocol letter to the defendants, essentially warning them of the potential claim, and outlining some of the circumstances surrounding it and the areas of negligence that would be cited. Following this, our solicitor began to work on developing the Particulars of the Claim. This document contains the specific details of the alleged medical negligence, and the amount of compensation that would be asked for, based on Rachel's past, current and ongoing needs.

This went back and forth between the various experts over many months and included further short reports from a variety of other clinical experts.

In 2002, as part of the process of gathering all the evidence for the Particulars of the Claim, a life expectancy report was prepared for Rachel. It concluded that, while Rachel could live until her mid-forties, it was highly likely that she would not survive into her 30s. It came up with a precise age of 27 as the age she might be expected to live to.

It's hard to explain how it feels to be told that your daughter is likely to die when she is 27 years old. At the time she was just 14. Of course, I knew she was never going to live as long as the average person, but back when she was a baby, Dr. G. had said there was no reason why she couldn't live well into late middle age. It was very upsetting and hard to take in.

Another big moment occurred in February, 2002, when, out of the blue, I received a letter from the Health Authority expressing their regret about what had happened to Rachel when she was born. They apologised for the fact that I had not received an acceptable standard of care during my labour. However, they stated they did not believe this had contributed to Rachel's cerebral palsy and disabilities. It was significant though. They were clearly scurrying around getting ready to defend themselves against our claim. Things were beginning to gather some momentum.

Coincidentally, but not unrelated, around this time our solicitors heard from the defence solicitors to the effect that, after extensive investigation, and even at this early stage, they were not of the opinion that any negligence had occurred on the part of the hospital. They admitted that there had been multiple "breaches of their duty of care" on their part, but that these had not caused Rachel's injuries.

They believed that Rachel's brain damage had occurred prior to my first attendance at hospital at 6pm on the day before her birth. This belief was based largely on an unlabeled recording of the baby's heart beat that they claimed was taken at 18:10 on my first admission on the 19th of May. This was consistent with Rachel having already suffered a "hypoxic injury" by this point. This was supported, in their opinion, by the fact that I had said I had not felt the baby move at all the day before she was born, and that the placenta was reported in the notes as being "gritty and infarcted" (a sign of possible poor blood flow to the baby).

I should note at this point, that I had not said I had felt *no* movements, only reduced movements (which is in fact normal in early labour), and that I remembered being told at the birth that the placenta was "healthy and intact". Besides, Rachel was a healthy size and weight for her age, so there was no evidence that she had been deprived of oxygen or nutrients in the womb due to placental insufficiency.

Equally, our experts fundamentally believed that the labour had been seriously mismanaged. Their interpretation of the 18:10 heart tracing was that it was not consistent with being taken before I was in established labour, as it clearly showed strong regular contractions that were linked to the dips in the baby's heart rate. I was definitely not experiencing contractions at 18:10.

It was a grossly abnormal tracing that showed periods of severe hypoxia that would have caused brain damage. My team was sure that the tracing was one that had been taken during my *second* admission, later that evening, when I *was* experiencing strong contractions. Because of the stage of her brain inflammation after the birth, as evidenced by ultrasound scans and blood tests, they believed that the brain damage occurred after midnight that night, and that, if an emergency caesarean section had been performed before midnight, Rachel's cerebral palsy could have been prevented.

The next stage of the process was to issue a Clinical Negligence Pre-Action Protocol to the defendants. This would contain as much detail as possible of the claim, including the history, the allegations, and the consequences of the negligence. It would also contain the final valuation of the claim, a detailed medical report, and all the other relevant supporting documentation. The aim of this communication was to give the defendants the opportunity to settle out of court and avoid incurring further costs on both sides. This was sent in May, 2002.

Following this, in June, the defendants responded by demanding that we take Rachel to be examined by one of their experts in Leeds. I explained that this would be difficult to arrange. It was not easy to take Rachel on long car journeys and be away from home for long periods, without somewhere we could change her nappy. In addition, due to her increasingly complex relationship with food, she would no longer eat or drink outside the home. It would be a long time for her to go without food or water.

I asked if it would be possible for him to come and examine her at home instead.

He refused.

I was furious and challenged it again. It seemed to me to be a completely unreasonable request in the circumstances, but they refused to back down. In the end, they said that if we refused to attend, they would apply to the court for a "stay" and the whole process would stop until the examination had been undertaken.

We were left with no choice but to make the trip. Steve drove us all up to Leeds on the 3rd of December, 2002. I cried all the way there, partly with frustration and distress for Rachel and partly with sheer fury. We were seen in his private clinic. We had to wait in the waiting area with all his other private patients. I was increasingly upset and tearful. Rachel picked up on all the tension too, and was shouting and generally making a scene. People stared at us. Others averted their eyes in awkward embarrassment. I was past caring. The whole thing was a complete nightmare.

To add insult to injury, when she was finally seen by the expert, he barely looked at her. We were in there for ten minutes at the most. He didn't physically examine her, simply looked her up and down and asked a couple of perfunctory questions that he could easily have asked over the phone. Steve and I were livid!

Throughout 2003, various other conferences and meetings took place. By now, Steve was coming with me to all these events. He was an enormous support to me. He never spoke or got involved, unless it was to make me take a "time out" when he could see I was becoming upset or anxious. He would just sit quietly by my side, but his presence alone, was both comforting and reassuring, and seemed to give me the strength I needed to get through these difficult times.

The experts continued to fine tune their opinions and reports, and we worked with the solicitors to prepare our witness statements. Letters and responses went back and forth. Several attempts to discuss a settlement out of court were made and rejected. The defendants asked for numerous extensions to give them time to gather statements and evidence, from the now extensive list of people involved, all of which resulted in further delays.

In 2004, it was decided by our team, that the opinion of yet another paediatric neurologist be sought, as our current expert in this field was still not fully supportive of Rachel's case. The solicitors had now approached over 20 different experts in their efforts to find one who was willing to help. When one was found, he then had to undertake his own review of the case and produce his own report. Again, this all had to go through all the usual Legal Aid hoops. The whole process was unbelievably slow.

Later in 2004, we received a copy of the full defence statement. In this, they made a full admission of a breach of duty of care from the moment I was admitted the first time on the day before Rachel's birth, right through to the second admission later that night and up until my discharge. They admitted that I should have received further monitoring and investigation, and that this would have led to Rachel's delivery by emergency caesarean section by 8pm on the 19th of May. However, they were still sticking to their claim that this would not have prevented Rachel's brain damage, as it had happened way before all that.

They also tried to claim that Rachel was not particularly unwell at birth, which was suggestive of a prolonged low-grade hypoxia, where the brain damage had occurred gradually over time, rather than an acute severe hypoxia resulting in acute extensive damage. They said that her Apgar score was good and that she did not require resuscitation. Our experts disputed this on the grounds of my own description of her condition, and the fact that that she was clearly poorly enough to justify an immediate admission to Special Care. In addition, the defence stated that she experienced only mild to moderate inflammation of her brain after the birth, whereas our experts pointed out that she was being treated for seizures within a few hours of her birth, which would suggest a much more serious degree of inflammation. In fact, the onset of these seizures was around midday on the day of her birth. Usually, swelling of the brain and symptoms of brain damage will occur 12 hours after the event, which would place the time of the damaging hypoxic injury at around midnight.

Finally, in September, 2004, 17 years after she was born, court proceedings were finally issued against the hospital where Rachel was born.

Chapter Fifteen – Different Stories

By January 2005, we were still waiting for a court date, the defendants having requested yet another extension. On our side, all the reports and financial estimates of the costs of Rachel's care had expired as they were over five years old, and they all had to be done again. But despite this, in anticipation of an imminent court case, we entered a new phase of flurried activity as final witness statements were taken, and all the expert reports were gathered together for the purpose of Disclosure, which is where all the documents that will be used in court are exchanged in advance between the different parties.

So much time seemed to have been wasted. It was so difficult for me to comprehend that almost 16 years had elapsed since my first approach to a solicitor. Rachel was now almost 18 – almost an adult who could benefit hugely from an early settlement. I could have allowed myself to become extremely frustrated by the length of time it had taken, but, over the years I'd learned - on JW's advice - to distract myself from the case. Otherwise, the process could have become an overwhelming drain on my mental wellbeing.

It was fascinating for me to hear the defendants' side of the story, and to see the medical notes after all these years, combined with the experts' opinions about what should have happened but didn't. At the same time, it was deeply disturbing to see how different their account of events was, compared to my own, and how many "breaches of duty of care" had actually occurred. I've already mentioned the conflicting descriptions of the placenta at birth, and the "reduced" versus "no" foetal movements, but there were a number of other discrepancies between the different versions of the story, and failures to follow good practice, which I will outline for you now.

When I was first admitted at 18:00 on the day before Rachel was born, the midwife was adamant that everything was fine. The monitor tracing that I recalled being taken showed no contractions at all, but did show the baby's heart rate slowing down from time to time. The midwife blamed it on the machine.

The medical records state that I was having some

tightenings (I was not), and that the heart rate was "reactive" at 140-160 beats per minute. The unlabelled tracing, which the defence claimed had been taken at that time, showed that I was in established labour and that the baby's heart rate was slowing significantly after each contraction. This raised some serious questions in my mind. If this was the case, why did they send me home? If, as they now claimed, this tracing was grossly abnormal and indicative that brain damage was already occurring, or had already occurred, why did they not perform an emergency caesarean section there and then?

I remember having five separate monitor tracings taken at different times:

Around 18:00 – when I was assessed and sent home.

Around 23:00 – on the Labour Ward, when I was re-admitted.

Around 01:00 – after I was transferred up to the ward.

Around 03:00 – on the ward, when I was told I was 5cm dilated.

Between 04:00 and the delivery at 08:00 – when I was back down on the Labour Ward.

After multiple requests over several years, only

four tracings eventually turned up. They were:

The unlabelled tracing which the defendants claimed was taken at 18:10.

One from 23:20 – on the Labour Ward when I was readmitted.

One from 03:00 – on the ward when I was 5cm dilated.

One from 04:00 - on the Labour Ward, which was intermittent until the delivery.

There was no tracing from when I was first transferred to the ward at 01:00. Our experts believed it to be highly plausible that the unlabelled tracing was actually the missing 01:00 tracing, because it showed regular, moderate contractions. This tracing, and the 23:30 one, both showed evidence of severe and damaging hypoxia that should have prompted an immediate emergency caesarean section.

It makes me feel sick to think that all of Rachel's disabilities might not have occurred if this had happened. Could it really have been that simple? Could all the years of heartache and suffering have really been prevented if one simple decision had been made? If they had delivered her by caesarian section as soon as the damage to her brain was beginning to occur? Sadly, I now believe this to be the case.

Although my solicitors never explicitly suggested this, I now believe that the real 18:10 tracing was deliberately "misplaced" and that the 01:00 one was deliberately "unlabelled" and substituted for the 18:10 one, to support the defence's case that the damage had occurred prior to my admission later on that night.

I hate to even consider this possibility, and I'm not blaming anyone in particular for the failures of care that occurred on that fateful night. But I am appalled that it appears they have added insult to injury by trying to cover up their mistakes. I find it hard to believe that any of the doctors and nurses involved in my care would deliberately do this, but there is no doubt in my mind that someone has done that ... and that makes me very sad indeed.

The discrepancies continued to back up my version of events.

When I was admitted later that night, the midwife was insistent that I wasn't in labour, but the medical records say that I was in early labour, and that I was being transferred to the ward to rest. Interestingly, as I was still only 36 weeks and 2 days pregnant, my baby would be defined as preterm, as it was under 37 weeks gestation. As such, it would be at increased risk of complications, including foetal hypoxia. In fact, the medical records stated, incorrectly, that I was 37 weeks and 3 days pregnant. When I was re-admitted after midnight, the records stated that I was 37 weeks and 4 days pregnant. So, no-one picked up that this was a premature labour, and I was not seen by a doctor as should have been the case. Maybe if a consultant had seen me at this stage, things might have turned out differently? I can't bear to think about it.

The monitor tracing that was taken at 23:20 was stated in the medical records as being reactive and therefore "normal", which in fact, it is not. It clearly shows dips in the baby's heart rate after the contractions, which is a sign of ongoing damaging hypoxia. This is undisputed. There is no doubt that this was missed by the midwife. I know they were very busy that night, and she was probably rushed off her feet, but if only she had taken the time to look at it properly, Rachel's life could have turned out so differently.

I believe that I was in established labour at this stage, not early labour, and this is borne out by the pattern of contractions on the tracings. The midwives admitted that they were busy and there was no room on the Labour Ward at the time. I was in pain and did ask for pain relief, but this was ignored. Instead, I was given some sleeping pills and transferred to the ward.

Even though I called the midwife several times between 01:00 and 03:00, because I was in pain, the next entry in my medical records was not until 02:45 when they note that I couldn't settle due to strong contractions, and they performed a vaginal examination. This showed that I was in established labour and 5cm dilated. Basically, I had got through the first stage of my labour alone … in the dark … with no pain relief. The notes do state that another tracing was commenced as the Labour Ward was full.

Again, perhaps if the nurse on the ward had taken me more seriously, and paid more attention to what I was saying, I would have been seen by the midwife sooner, and someone would have realised that something was wrong.

My distressing memories of being taken down to the Labour Ward at about 04:00 were confirmed by the medical records. I still had not received any pain relief. That agonizing journey haunts me to this day. I honestly believed my baby and I were going to die. I was in so much pain and distress.

From then on, as I remember it, I was very much left on my own. Apart from Giles arriving and my being put on the monitor again, I barely saw anyone. This is backed up to a degree by the medical notes which show very few recordings of the labour, apart from a poor quality and intermittent monitor tracing. All the charts and observations that would usually take place in labour do not appear to have been done in my case. This part is all the more frustrating because I remember how Giles and I were so convinced by now that something was seriously wrong. I lost count of the number of times we pressed the buzzer to ask for pain relief and reassurance that our baby was ok. If only someone had listened.

I don't recall anyone coming in to see us until about 07:00, when everything then seemed to happen very quickly, given that Rachel was born at 08:00. I was examined, my waters were broken, and I was finally given pain relief, all I believe, between 07:00 and 07:30. I distinctly remember being asked to push almost immediately after I was given an injection of pethidine. I know this, because I was so relieved to finally receive pain relief, albeit almost eight hours after my first request.

In contrast, the medical records state that I was seen and examined at 05:30 because I was requesting pain relief, and that this was administered at 06:10. They also state that the doctor was called at 06:00 because the waters were stained with meconium (the contents of an unborn baby's bowels and another sign of foetal distress), and the baby's heart rate was slowing after each contraction.

Even the time of birth is different to my own. I recall Rachel being born at exactly 08:00 but the medical records say that this occurred at 07:50. You might be inclined to think that the time of birth stated in the medical records has to be correct. In reply, I would say that the time your first child is born is not a time you are likely to forget or get confused about, especially if they are born exactly on the hour as Rachel was.

I remember Rachel being silent, blue and floppy for a long time after she was born. I remember them working on her on the other side of the room and how concerned everyone appeared to be. I remember seeing her for a fleeting moment, before she was whisked away to Special Care. The Apgar score is a test that is performed on all babies at birth to assess their health and wellbeing. The medical records state that Rachel had an Apgar score of 7 out of 10 at one minute, and 9 out of 10 at five minutes. They also state that she required Narcan to counteract the effects of the pethidine. Again, this doesn't add up to me. If I had had the pethidine at 06:10, would she still have been affected by it? If I had had it 30 minutes before the birth, this would have been more understandable.

I'm sorry to say, that, for me, the medical records

of what happened in the last stages of my labour, are a complete fabrication, which bears little or no resemblance to my own memories of the experience. I have no choice but to believe that the medical records were either written up after the event to make them look better than they actually were, especially as best practice had clearly not been followed, and Rachel had been admitted to Special Care. Or, that they may have been "altered" during the years when they were alleged to be "missing".

Interestingly, the last monitor tracing ends at 07:57, seven minutes after they claim that Rachel was born but 3 minutes before I recall her being born. Need I say more?

Our medical experts suggested that, during my labour, many things didn't happen that should have. I should have been monitored more closely and been seen by a doctor sooner. A foetal scalp electrode should have been applied to get a more accurate reading of the baby's heart rate. Blood samples should have been taken from the baby. I should not have been given pethidine, as it is contraindicated in premature labour; I should have been offered an epidural instead. At the end of the labour, I should have been given an episiotomy to hasten the birth, because the baby was showing obvious signs of distress.

It is shocking to me that there were so many

failings on the part of the hospital in relation to my care.

If, as I believe, they were so busy that night that they simply did not have time to look after me properly, and they were taken by surprise by the fact that my labour had progressed so quickly, it could explain why so many of these things didn't happen. But it does not explain why, in my opinion, they tried to cover it up and refused to accept any responsibility for what happened.

Ultimately, though, there is no doubt in my mind, nor those of my entire legal team, that Rachel should have been delivered by caesarean section as soon as I was re-admitted to the hospital at 23:00 on the 19th of May.

In addition to everything else I have mentioned, there are places in the notes where other things appear to have been altered or added - that is to say, where things seem to have been entirely deleted, or erased and re-written. As a result, I have a strong suspicion that the notes were not "lost" for all those years, but were actually being "tidied up" to reflect their own version of events.

What was even more upsetting, though, was the

fact that my own legal team and all the medical experts seemed to favour the medical records' account over my own. They politely ignored my assertions that the story they told was not the way I remembered it. They suggested that it was all so long ago ... that I might have forgotten the details of what happened. I suppose it was easier for them to stick to what they believed to be the facts. If they accepted my claim that the notes had been "altered", it would open another massive can of legal worms which they were trying to avoid. Their job was to win the case as soon as possible. It had already taken 16 years to get to this stage. If we threw falsification of medical records into the mix, maybe it would go on for another 16!

Nevertheless, I know that my version of events is correct. Of course, you forget some things after 14 years. But you never forget being left alone in the dark and in pain, afraid to press the buzzer until the next 15 minutes is up ... focused on your watch as the seconds and minutes slowly tick by. You never forget being wheeled down a hospital corridor in agony, all the time thinking you and your baby are going to die. You never forget spending most of your first labour on your own, watching your baby's heart rate drop for minutes at a time, only to be told that it is down to faulty equipment. You never forget the hours of sheer torture, asking again and again for pain relief which never comes.

Whatever the medical notes say and whatever the legal teams, all those involved, and you the reader choose to believe, I own my own truth.

In May, 2005, shortly before Rachel's 18th birthday, a court date was set for Monday, the 24th of April, 2006. It was a huge relief, to finally see an end in sight after everything we had been through. But the relief was tinged with anger and frustration that it had taken 16 years to get to this point, and it would still take almost another year before it was finally resolved.

Chapter Sixteen – Rachel turns 18

On the 20th of May, 2005, Rachel turned 18. My beautiful baby daughter, who I was told might not survive the night on the day she was born, was now an adult.

We had a huge party. Everybody came to celebrate her special birthday. The day was filled with fun and laughter, and more presents than she had ever seen. She loved every minute of it. She still adored parties and being the centre of attention. She shone in her blue prom-style dress, as David pushed her around and around the dance floor in her wheelchair to the sounds of Abba, her favourite group, blaring from the stage. We'd hired a tribute band for the evening and I honestly believe she thought that the real group had turned up just to sing for her on her 18th birthday.

For every child, the day they become an adult is the start of a new and exciting phase of their lives. Similarly, for Rachel, becoming an adult represented the start of a new phase, too. Apart from anything else, the fact that she had made it to the age of 18 was a miracle in itself, and that of course was a cause for celebration. But becoming an adult was also a turning point for Rachel, which was going to prove more difficult than we could ever imagine.

Rachel was starting life as a profoundly disabled adult. She was no longer a cute little, blue-eyed, curly-haired baby in a pushchair. She was now a fully grown woman, who could not sit up unaided, use her hands in any purposeful movements, roll herself over or change her position, walk or weight-bear for transfer, speak or communicate in any consistent way, eat or drink unaided. She also required all of her food to be pureed, and was doubly incontinent.

Rachel still had a complex relationship with food. She was very self-conscious about eating and drinking, and would refuse to eat or drink outside the home. Whenever she was upset or anxious, she expressed this by refusing to eat, often leading to hospital admissions with dehydration and severe constipation.

Now that she was an adult, she could no longer be cared for by the wonderful Dr. G. and could not be treated at the Children's Hospital. She was now under the care of several different adult consultants for different aspects of her care. When she was admitted as an emergency, she would be taken to whichever hospital could take her on the day, often involving long waits on trolleys in corridors and A&E departments. She would be admitted onto adult wards under the care of people who didn't know her or understand her needs.

Some of these admissions were extremely stressful for all involved. Sometimes she would end up on one of the overcrowded, 30-plus-bedded, mixed gender, assessment wards. If she was luckier, she would be on a regular ward in a bay designed for either 2, 4 or 8 people. From a noise perspective, the 2-person bays were preferable but they were small and cramped, which made adequately caring for her physical needs almost impossible. But the larger bays, where we had more room to manoeuvre around her bed, could be very noisy. Rachel is hypersensitive to noise. She has never lost the startle reflex that we all possess as newborn babies but grow out of as we get older. Any unexpected noise will make her flinch violently, and almost jump out of her skin.

In addition, due to the "frog" position of her legs as a result of her hip surgery, a typical, single size hospital bed with rail sides, is completely unsuitable for Rachel, as her knees 'jar' against the sides, causing bruising and pressure sores.

As well as all this, many of the hospital staff, from consultant level to care assistant, are nervous around her, clearly uncomfortable with her disabilities. Some of them are unable to hide their shock at the extent of her physical problems, and others have even made unkind and hurtful comments.

So, an adult hospital ward is not really the ideal environment for Rachel. It is much better for her, and far easier for us, to look after her at home, where she is in familiar surroundings and has all the necessary equipment. However, while we clearly try to avoid admissions to hospital at all costs, there are, of course, times when this is just not possible.

As well as moving into the adult healthcare system, she also moved from child to adult social care. When she was 19, she would have to leave school and utilise whatever was available to her in terms of adult social care services.

School for Rachel was not about her receiving an education and qualifications that would enable her to get a job in the future. It was her social life and part of her care network, and a key part of our family support system. We were about to have all of this taken away. so, I was really worried about what this aspect of Rachel's future would hold for us all.

We had a meeting at the school with her teachers and her new adult social worker to plan for her leaving school, and to discuss her needs and the options available to her. The new social worker turned up late and was completely unprepared.

A few minutes into the meeting she looked at her and said, "Rachel doesn't have much to say for herself, does she?"

It didn't bode well for our ongoing relationship with her, that she clearly knew nothing about Rachel. We were entering a whole new world of over-stretched and underfunded adult services. We genuinely feared for her future.

As one social worker put it, "Now she is competing with all the little old ladies down the road."

It was rapidly beginning to feel as though our familiar, little world was collapsing around us and the rafters had caught alight.

By now, Steve and I had become engaged. We had started our own landscaping business; I dealt with the administrative aspects, and he covered the operational side. He had also moved in with me and the girls. He had two sons of his own, who didn't live with him but visited regularly. They got on well with Katie and Brooke. Rachel seemed to enjoy the extra chaos this brought to our home and would sit in her specialised armchair giggling at all her siblings' antics.

Rachel continued to go into respite every other week. On those weeks, we would take her there in time for Sunday lunch and pick her up after tea on the following Sunday. On the weeks she was at home, she would attend school on weekdays. Her epilepsy remained a problem, and she still required occasional admissions when it was uncontrolled. It was easier to predict when she was going to have a seizure, though. As she got older, she seemed to have developed some sort of inner warning system – it could almost be described as an aura - which would cause her to scream in fear and distress. Although it was always an upsetting experience, it enabled us to administer the rescue medication before things spiralled out of control.

When she was at home, we had a night carer who worked from 8pm until 8am every day except Friday and Saturday, funded by social services. They would help get her ready for school in the mornings during term time. We had another carer, funded by the charity that had supported us all through her life, who would be there when she got home from school until 8.30pm every day. In the school holidays, this carer would work from 10am to help out during the daytime.

Although this care was necessary, and I'm not sure how we would have coped without it, it also presented its own problems due to the size and layout of our home. The full impact of having a carer within your home is difficult to explain unless you've actually experienced it. When you have a relatively small kitchen and only one sitting room, which the whole family is trying to use, any degree of privacy is impossible. You have to learn to live with this, but nevertheless, it represents a significant intrusion into family life. But, of course, this inconvenience is far outweighed by the invaluable help we received.

Much as we all loved the respite facility, I was beginning to feel that it would be better for Rachel to be at home with us full-time once she left school. As well as the fact that she was going to lose all the support she got at school. I was becoming aware that she was not as happy there as she had been in the past. As she got older, she loved to be with the rest of the family and became increasingly upset when we left her on alternate Sunday evenings. When we arrived to pick her up, she seemed desperate to get home, refusing to finish her meal if she was still being fed when we arrived.

But, having Rachel at home full-time, was just not possible with the level of support we were currently receiving, particularly with her being about to leave school. She received a lot of sensory stimulation and physical therapies at school and also in respite, which we couldn't provide at home. In order for me to be able to continue to work, run the house and look after the other two girls, we would need a small army of full-time carers. Although its recommendations were never fully implemented, a risk assessment by social services had concluded that she required two carers at all times, due to the degree of lifting and handling involved.

While ceiling track hoists had been installed when the extension had been built to make it easier to transfer her between her bedroom and bathroom, we just didn't have the space in our current home, nor the funding, to create the holistic environment that she needed. It was a precarious situation. We couldn't provide everything she needed within our own home, but due to my concerns that Rachel had stopped enjoying respite, this troubled me. They had wonderful facilities and equipment that were fantastic for her physical needs, but just as importantly she also had emotional needs, which could only be met by being surrounded by the love of her family.

And so, we decided to try and find a way of providing her with everything she currently got at school and in respite, at home. The first step towards making this happen was to move to a bigger and more suitable property.

So, Steve and I began to explore the possibility of selling both of our homes and buying a bigger house that could accommodate all of our family: the two of us and all of our children, including his boys whenever they came to stay. We needed somewhere that would enable Rachel to be with us full-time. Ideally, we would need a property that had a ground floor space that could be adapted into a suite for her, her carers and her therapists, with a bedroom, bathroom and sitting area. A large bungalow would work best as it would afford Rachel access to the rest of the house so that she could easily integrate with the rest of the family. Because we had already had a grant to adapt our existing home, we were not entitled to another, and would have to fund the entire project ourselves

We started looking around for a suitable property. It wasn't easy! Our budget and search criteria were so limited. In addition, our search area was governed by Rachel's care package, because if we were to move out of the local council district, she would lose the care she was receiving, and we would have to start the assessment process all over again. It was so frustrating as we found a number of properties that were suitable, but fell outside of the area, and the date for her to leave school was rapidly approaching.

In the meantime, the court date was approaching. Everyone was gearing up for it: polishing up their statements and reports, and double-checking that everything was complete and up to date.

We, along with all the experts, had been told to set aside 10 working days for the case. I was both nervous and excited at the same time. The moment we had been building up to for 18 years was almost upon us. The fact that an end to the struggle was in sight, whatever the outcome, was a release in itself.

I had never been inside a courtroom before. I'd only ever seen them in films or on the TV. And we weren't going to just any old court. We were going to the biggest and most prestigious court in the country: The Royal Courts of Justice!

However, the legal team kept stressing that, even at this late stage, it still might not come to that. There was always a chance that they might decide to settle out of court, and this could happen right up to the last minute. It was not unheard of for this to happen on the courtroom steps!

It was so difficult to remain calm, knowing that, finally, we were going to get closure on all the unresolved questions and issues that surrounded Rachel's case. I could hardly wait.

The legal process was beginning to feel like one great big game of "chicken" - a test to see which side would blink first. We had been advised that, if we won in court, we could expect to receive compensation to the tune of between £4 and £5 million. However, there was no guarantee that we would win, and we could walk away with nothing. The NHS had a big enough purse to employ the best lawyers in the country. They also had robust and complex insurance policies in place, and any compensation settlements were paid through these, and not taken from NHS funds designated for patient care.

The defence were testing to see if I was really prepared to take the stand and risk walking away with nothing, and my team were testing to see if they were brave enough to risk having to pay out the millions that might be involved if we went to court and won. It was an annoying process, but I knew we had to get on and play the game. There was no choice for me.

Looking back, I really feel that our whole medical negligence system in the UK is in need of a serious overhaul. In Sweden, for instance, they have a system whereby if you are injured through medical negligence, they have a mechanism in place, which provides compensation without proof of provider fault. A system like this would have meant Rachel would have received whatever she needed from a very young age, without the need to go through a prolonged and expensive litigation process.

Our team was preparing to start the process of coaching me on how to behave in court: what to say and what not to say. We had a "trial run" planned, when they would question me and "put me through the mill" in a worst-case scenario mock-up of the "cross-examination under oath" experience.

I didn't care. I couldn't wait for it all to be over. I was fully prepared to give Rachel the best chance of a successful outcome. In my heart, I truly believed that she would finally get the justice she deserved, and I would finally be able to let go of any last shreds of personal guilt. I never once questioned my judgement on whether this was the right thing to do.

Then, out of the blue, the judge ordered that we all had one last meeting to try again to reach a settlement. A meeting was set up in the barrister's chambers on the 24th of March, 2006, exactly a month before the court date. Never was the "game" more apparent than on that day. The QC, whom we met for the first time, and our barrister were like a couple of excited public schoolboys. I was genuinely shocked! Here were some of the most highly respected, highly qualified, and highly paid, legal dignitaries in the country, giggling and running around like toddlers playing with a puppy. I just watched their faces in bemused silence.

I was accompanied by Steve, Giles, and Rachel's solicitor, JW. We were shown into a large boardroom and seated at a big oval table, then the QC explained what was going to happen. The defence were in a similar room in another part of the building. Every effort was made to ensure that neither party met each other. The day began with the QC and the barrister delivering their opening statements to the defence, and vice versa. We were not permitted to witness these opening statements, which were the same ones that they would use in court if we couldn't reach an agreement at this meeting. As the QC spoke, I began to tremble. The enormity of the day hit me in a tsunami of emotions. Steve placed his arm protectively on the back of my seat, behind my neck.

Following this, both sides were given time to consider their positions. The QC explained that, based on the defence's case, he believed we only had a 60% chance of winning and we should bear this in mind when considering any offers they might make. The odds were disappointing, but I remained calm, as I knew this was just his opinion and he was still prepared to fight them in court if it came to it, whatever the odds. Steve, Giles, and I had discussed our strategy beforehand and they were both adamant that the final decision on acceptance of any settlement fee should be mine and mine alone, as Rachel's mother and representative.

But it wasn't about the money for me. Of course, the money would make a huge difference to Rachel's life, but more than anything I just wanted the defence to admit to me, once and for all, that none of this was my fault - that I'd done nothing wrong.

After a while, the defence came back in to tell us that they had brought "no purse" with them and were not in a position to make a settlement of any kind. The QC said that was fine and we would just have to take it to court. We were all packing up to leave when they appeared at the door again. The QC and barrister went off to talk to them while we all wondered what was happening. When the pair returned, their excitement had reached fever pitch. They couldn't wait to tell us that we had been offered a settlement of £500,000. They were ecstatic.

I looked at them coldly. I didn't consider accepting it for a second. Really? £500,000 for all the damage they had done to Rachel. It was ridiculous. An insult.

I spoke to the QC.

"Go straight back in and tell them we'll see them in court."

He opened his mouth to speak, but I stopped him.

"Go now! The longer you take, the more likely they are going to think I'm considering it!"

They looked surprised, then glanced at each other and quickly left the room. I sat quietly and waited, grappling with my emotions. I had to keep a clear head and not allow them to cloud my judgement.

They returned a few minutes later with an offer of £1 million. I immediately declined again. Compared to the £4 or £5 million she might get in court, it still seemed like an unreasonable offer. Besides, I knew that this sum was based on an estimate of her expected future care needs. I tried to remember costs in my head adding everything up:, future care costs, all the future equipment she may need, a suitable house and all the refurbishment costs, the extra care if we decided not to send her to respite anymore. My mind was racing. Was it enough?

This time the QC questioned my judgment.

"Mrs. Taylor, think about what you are doing. We have a million pounds on the table here. Think what this money might mean for Rachel and her future. Think what you are denying her by refusing it on her behalf. We could go to court and lose it all."

I looked at him. I didn't know what to do.

He spoke again. "Why don't the three of you go for a walk and think about it? You must be sure you are making the right decision. For Rachel."

We did as he suggested. We went for a walk. It

was a beautiful spring day. The chambers looked out over a traditional, leafy London square. The blossom was out, and the air smelt fresh and clean. Only the distant sounds of traffic in the streets beyond, reminded us that we were in the heart of the city.

Steve and Giles were steadfast in their resolve that it was up to me to make the decision. They didn't try to influence me in any way.

I kept remembering a story that Rachel's physio had told me, about someone who had gone through a similar experience. They had waited until the third offer before they accepted. I made up my mind. I was going to hold out for one third and final offer. I was sure they were going to make it, but if they didn't, we still had the court to fall back on.

The third offer came through at £1.5 million, and I accepted.

A wave of relief washed over me. They had finally admitted what they had done. The money they had awarded Rachel proved that. They had finally been called to account. They had caused the injury to Rachel's brain, not me.

But, at the same time, I couldn't believe it was over. Eighteen years of going back and forth to see solicitors, which had become part of our lives.

Eighteen years of being rallied, soothed, coaxed and sometimes provoked by our legal and medical teams. Eighteen years of legal jargon and piles of paperwork. Eighteen years of trying to remain sweet-tempered and calm, and patient even though at times I wanted to scream and shout at them. Eighteen years of wondering where it would all end, if indeed it ever would. Eighteen years of sheer perseverance.

But the QC explained that it still wasn't quite over. We would still have to go to court to have the settlement approved by the judge. It was expected to be a formality, but it wasn't time to celebrate just yet.

A few weeks later we were back in London, at the Royal Courts of Justice for the judge's approval. It was an overwhelming experience. Again, Steve and Giles were there to support me. Our solicitor had explained that I would have to take the stand to answer any questions that the judge might have. I was terrified. As we approached the imposing pale grey, gothic façade, I was aware that I was trembling again. Again, Steve's touch was there to steady me.

But, in the end, it was a swift and straightforward conclusion to what had been a tortuous 18-year journey. The Family Court where our case was heard was a bright and modern space. Nothing like the austere formal setting that I had imagined. I was still trembling when I took the stand, but the questions were simple confirmations of some of the details. The judge approved the settlement, and it was done.

Now, it was over. We'd done it. We had won. We had secured enough funding for all of Rachel's future care needs. She had finally got justice for what had happened to her.

Now, we could finally put the past behind us and move forward as a family.

Giles made his own way home, and Steve and I headed for the nearest bar for a large glass of wine. Later, he took me shopping in Hatton Garden, where he bought me a bracelet to celebrate, and afterwards, we stayed in town for the night. But before all that, we had to ring home and warn my parents that the press might go to the house, and not to answer the door to anyone. Rachel was away in respite, but my parents were at home looking after the two younger girls.

When we had arrived, our solicitor had told us that the press might be in the court, but if we didn't want to talk to them, we should just leave quickly and quietly without speaking to anyone. We didn't want to talk and had taken her advice, but she drew our attention to the fact that our address had been read out in court, and they might turn up at our home.

And they did.

They rang the doorbell and pushed their business cards through the letterbox. We ignored all their requests for us to share our story, but they ran it anyway. The following day, our settlement was front page news in all the local papers. The numbers were splashed across the top of the page for all the world to see.

People we hadn't heard from in years started calling us to say how pleased they were for us. Parents at the school approached me to ask all about it. Whilst I hadn't solicited the attention and didn't really enjoy it, it still felt right that our victory was being recognised and appreciated for what it was.

It was a wonderful time. The end of the longest battle I had ever fought on Rachel's behalf. But, despite it all, when the dust settled, and I really had time to think about it, I felt, and still do, a little cheated that we never had a full explanation as to what had actually gone wrong, and why.

And most of all, we had never had a formal apology for how they had let us down.

Chapter Seventeen – A New Chapter

Whilst we had won the biggest battle of our lives, of course, that was not the end of Rachel's story. It was actually the beginning of a new and exciting chapter for all of us.

The money made a huge difference to our lives, as we were now secure in the knowledge that Rachel's care needs would be met for the rest of her life, whatever the future had in store.

As I got older, and Rachel continued to defy all the predictions about her life expectancy, I had begun to seriously consider the possibility that she might outlive me. I was very conscious that I did not want Rachel's sisters to find themselves in a position where the responsibility and financial burden of her care might fall on them. Now that I knew this would almost certainly never happen, it gave me great peace of mind.

But the first thing on our agenda was a wedding!

At this point, Steve and I had been engaged for over a year and, even before we knew about the court date, had been planning our wedding for June the 2nd, 2007. Now, with the legal battles behind us, we could properly celebrate and enjoy the occasion. My three girls were to be my bridesmaids, Steve's boys, our ushers, and Louise, my maid of honour.

It was a joyous day. The ceremony and the reception took place at a beautiful old manor house hotel near Coventry. The sun shone down on us as we made our vows surrounded by our family and friends. I couldn't remember when I had last felt so happy. The next day my face ached from smiling and laughing. Rachel loved every minute of it. Life had never felt better.

The conditions of Rachel's settlement meant that we were still entitled to the part-time care package from the local authority, and the charity would continue to donate their hours. But now, we were able to top this up with her own money to provide her with round-the-clock care in the home environment. We could take her out of respite and arrange for her to have all the additional therapies that she received both there and at school, which made such a difference to her quality of life. These included regular aromatherapy and massage to ease her painful muscle spasms.

But we still needed a bigger and more suitable

home to be able to do this, and to accommodate our new extended family, so, our search for a new home was resumed in earnest. Steve had already sold his property and planned to use the money from this sale to fund any renovations that would inevitably be required.

It wasn't long before we found a dormer bungalow that was perfect in terms of its structure and layout. But it was run down and neglected and would need a lot of work to make it habitable. We had a long and honest discussion about whether we could take it on and still care for Rachel and the girls, as well as managing our landscaping business. The timing of the purchase meant that the work would take place over the autumn and winter when the business was quieter, and Steve was confident that he would have time to oversee the project. We would continue to live in my house until it was ready for us all to move in.

But, ironically, the day we picked up the keys in early September coincided with our securing the biggest landscaping contract we had ever had! Steve was going to be busier than he had ever been, and it was going to be impossible for him to manage the renovation project, too. I therefore had no choice but to step in and take charge.

It was a daunting project. I had never done anything like it before and was on a near-vertical learning curve. The whole interior of the property had to be re-plastered and re-decorated; it needed re-wiring, new doors and floors throughout, and Rachel's rooms had to be adapted to facilitate her care needs, with a hoist and accessible bathroom, and a sitting area for her and her carers.

In the end, I found it one of the most rewarding things I had ever done. We had set ourselves the goal of moving in by Christmas, and on Christmas Eve, the finishing touches were still being completed. Wooden floors were being installed in the hallway and the plumber was completing some of his work.

At one point, he managed to set fire to one of the walls with his blow torch, and if it hadn't been for Steve's quick thinking and bravery in terms of putting out the fire with his bare hands, the whole house could have burnt down! But it didn't, and we were all able to move in late on Christmas Eve, even though there was still a huge hole in one of the walls.

It was a wonderful Christmas with the whole family together for the first time. My girls had their own room, Steve's boys had theirs, and Rachel had her own spacious suite with a sitting room for her and her carers. The house was set up so that she had her own private space but could be easily wheeled into any of the rooms on the ground floor to be with the rest of the family. It was perfect. That Christmas was one of the happiest I can remember.

The only parts of the house that were upstairs

and away from all the hustle and bustle were Steve's and my bedroom and the boy's room.

Steve and I were overjoyed to have our own bedroom and bathroom in the dormer area of the house. I've touched before on how difficult it is having carers in the house 24 hours a day. The lack of privacy can be incredibly stressful. I can only compare it to living in a goldfish bowl. In the old house, the carers needed access to all of the living areas of the property, but in the new house, this was largely limited to Rachel's suite and the kitchen and laundry areas. They had their privacy and we had ours. It was better for everyone.

Once we were settled in, we decided it was time to take Rachel out of respite. Although they had been absolutely wonderful with her and the family for so many years, it felt like the right time for many different reasons. Rachel was an adult now and had different needs and desires. As I have mentioned previously, she didn't seem to be as happy there as she had been when she was younger.

The decision was one of the best we ever made. We had wanted to have Rachel at home with the rest of the family full-time, and still provide her with everything she needed, and now we could.

For a while, life was almost idyllic. The legal fight was over, Rachel was home full-time with 24-hour care, we had enough space for the whole family, and we had more privacy than we had ever experienced. Personally, I was in a really good place. As well as being in a loving relationship for the first time in years, I had also finally let go of some of the guilt that I had been carrying for so long ... guilt about what had happened to Rachel and my part in that, and guilt about not being able to give her the level of care, in her own home, that I believed she deserved.

How foolish of me, though, to allow myself to think that all our battles were behind us and that life would be simple from then on.

Once Rachel's settlement was approved, we were surprised to learn that the money would not be paid into an account in her name, but into a special account at the Court Funds Office, where it would be managed through a body called The Court of Protection. This meant that she was not able to take advantage of optimal market interest rates and would be subject to a number of different administration fees.

At first, this did not seem to be too much of a problem, and she was receiving a 6% interest rate. But after the "crash" in 2008, this dropped to 0.5%. We could have accessed more competitive rates if we had been allowed to move the money out, but this was forbidden by the court. Her pot soon began to dwindle.

The Court of Protection itself creates an interesting situation that is not without its own challenges. As Rachel's mother, I have been subject to a stream of different court orders over time, which detail what I am, and what I am not, permitted to do on her behalf. Every court order and every significant action that I take, or attempt to take, for her must be approved by the court and incurs a fee that is taken directly from her funds. It has been an expensive business.

The first court order was put in place in July, 2006, and incurred an "appointment fee" of £330. This required me to maintain and submit annual accounts in relation to the use of Rachel's funds. The second court order was issued on the 14th of August, 2007, and granted me the position of "receiver" for Rachel's affairs. This allowed me to, for the next 3 years, withdraw up to £70,000 a year on her behalf. I could deposit her funds into new accounts in her name, including ISAs. I could also use her money to make charitable donations and purchase Christmas and birthday gifts for family and close friends, as long as they were for a reasonable amount. I was not allowed to execute a will or settlement, conduct any legal proceedings, sell or purchase any property, or employ a solicitor or other professional on her behalf. All these things had to be done by the court.

The third and final court order, and the one that is still in place today, appointed me as her official decision making "deputy". This allows me to manage her affairs more freely, but any decisions I make on her behalf are still subject to several restrictions. For example, I cannot sell, lease, or charge any property that she owns or has a share in, and any gifts, donations or provisions must be deemed "reasonable" by the court.

I was required to obtain the advice of an FSA-regulated financial adviser within three months of the order, and obtain a security bond for £450,000. I am, to this day, required to maintain detailed and accurate financial records of Rachel's accounts and submit an annual report to the Public Guardian.

Whilst this gave me more freedom to manage Rachel's affairs in a way that was in her best interests, and gave her the best return on her money, it is still very tightly controlled and incurs significant administration costs. She is required to pay an annual administration fee of £330, and the cost of the security bond is £900 a year. In addition, any application to the court for anything that falls outside of the order incurs a charge of £385.

I understand that its purpose is to protect Rachel's assets from misuse and worse. But, as someone who is committed to ensure that her money is always used only for her needs, it is a frustrating arrangement at times. In particular, it galls me that so much of the money that is intended for her care is being eaten away by the costs of managing the fund.

However, even more difficult times were ahead. In the September of 2008, a couple of years after the settlement and a few months after Rachel's 21st birthday, my father was diagnosed with terminal cancer. His health had been poor for the 12 months prior to this, as he had developed dementia. For the last few months of his life, my mother decided that she wanted to nurse him at home, with the support of the local Macmillan team.

It was a sad time for us all, but Rachel seemed to take it harder than everyone. She had always had a special bond with my father, and they were very close. At the same time as he was ill, her own health began to deteriorate. She began to exhibit some of the same signs and symptoms that he had. When he had thrush in his mouth, she got it too, when he was in pain, she seemed to be in pain, as well. It was all very strange and extremely disconcerting.

Ultimately, she expressed her grief in the only way she knew - by refusing to eat or drink. (Incidentally, my father had also stopped eating and drinking at the same time.) This time, for Rachel, it was worse than ever. She soon became severely dehydrated, extremely constipated and her seizures were out of control, as she was not taking her medication. We had no choice but to call an ambulance and get her admitted to hospital.

I was horrified when the paramedics told me we

were going to the hospital where she was born. This was the first time we had been there since her birth, 21 years earlier. It took all my mental strength and focus not to flip into a full-blown flashback and panic attack. Steve came with us, as he knew how difficult it was going to be, and he never left my side throughout the whole ordeal.

Rachel was admitted from A&E into a general ward. The staff all seemed uncomfortable around her, and I subsequently discovered that they were aware of our legal case with the hospital. It was stamped in red letters all over her notes. No-one seemed willing to take responsibility for her care. They couldn't decide which "category" she fell under and which consultant she should be looked after by.

Rachel was as poorly as I had ever seen her. Deathly pale and unresponsive. Her usually bright blue eyes were dull, and her skin was sallow and drawn across her cheekbones. I truly believed that we might be finally about to lose her. I couldn't believe that, after everything that had happened to us, she was going to die here, 21 years after she was born in the very same hospital. That couldn't be the end of her story. I wouldn't allow it.

But 24 hours after she was admitted, she had still not been treated. They had been unable to insert a cannula to give her IV fluids, or insert a naso-gastric tube to give her nourishment and medication. She still had not been seen by a doctor after she had left A&E. All the other patients had the name of their consultant on a sign above their bed. Rachel's was blank.

Thirty-six hours passed. I could see her deteriorating before my eyes. It honestly seemed as though they were just going to let her fade away. I was distraught.

Eventually, Steve decided to take matters into his own hands. He'd had enough. He walked up to the nurse's station and demanded to know which doctor was going to be managing Rachel's care. He refused to be fobbed off or take no for an answer. He stood there until they had made a few phone calls and came back with a name.

"Mr. [P.], should be Rachel's consultant," the nurse said.

"Where is he now?" Steve asked.

"He'll be running an outpatient's clinic downstairs," she replied.

I watched as Steve walked through the double doors and disappeared into the corridor beyond.

I don't know exactly what happened in that clinic, but Steve told me later that he had knocked on the door of the consultant's office calmly and politely, and asked him when he would be able to come and see our daughter, because we were afraid that she was dying. He had refused to come immediately stating that he was in the middle of a clinic.

Steve had then addressed all the patients in the waiting room and told them, "Clinic is over. The consultant is required upstairs on the ward to see my daughter, who is dying."

Security was called, but Steve wouldn't budge until Mr. P assured him that he would attend to Rachel as soon as his clinic was finished, and no later than 6pm.

A very courteous Mr. P. arrived at 6pm, and an intravenous infusion was finally started to try and re-hydrate her.

The next few weeks were a blur of hospital visits and visits to my father. Rachel was still in hospital when he passed away on the 21st of November. She grieved for him for a very long time. After she was eventually discharged from the local hospital, she had several readmissions over the next six months. I was reluctant for her to go back there and, more often than not, we ended up in another hospital closer to the city centre. While I had more confidence in the care she received there, it was not the best environment in which to look after her. It was an old Victorian building and space was limited. Although they usually gave us a two-bedded room to ourselves, there was still not enough space to move easily around the bed to wash and change her.

I felt as though we were trapped in a vicious cycle of her refusing to eat and drink, being admitted for IV fluids and naso-gastric feeding, returning home, and then her refusing to eat or drink again. I was at my wits' end and couldn't see a workable solution. At the same time, I was grieving for the father I had loved so much, and who had been such a big part of my life.

But this all changed when, in March, 2009, we met a special young doctor who, it emerged, had trained under the wonderful Dr. G. He took a special interest in Rachel's case. Sadly, he told us that Dr. G. had passed away, but it was a great testament to him to see that some of his knowledge and passion had rubbed off on his protégé.

The doctor suggested that we consider having Rachel fitted with a permanent Balloon Gastrostomy Tube (BGT), which would allow her to be fed directly into her stomach. The procedure had to be approved by a medical panel, but, with his support, it went through and she had it fitted just a few days later.

The BGT transformed all of our lives. Rachel received all her medication, hydration, and nourishment in the form of liquid food supplements, through the tube. She began to thrive again. She gained weight, and her strength and smile returned. Her epilepsy was well-controlled as she was receiving the correct dose of medication every day through the tube. We continued to offer her puréed food by mouth and she gradually began to accept this. After about 12 months, she was eating three puréed meals a day, and we only used the BGT for additional hydration fluids and her oral medication.

By now, Rachel was receiving all her care, and all her therapies, at home. Our vision of caring for her full-time at the heart of the family had been realised, and it was working well for everyone. Rachel was happy and content and recovered from her bout of ill health, and we were loving having her at home where she belonged.

Chapter Eighteen – Life Today

So here we are in 2020, in the middle of a global pandemic, and Rachel has survived, and thrived, against all the odds.

During lockdown she celebrated her 33rd birthday and has left her predicted life expectancy of 27 far behind her. It's not been easy over the past few months. She has been "shielding" and we have had to cancel many of her usual therapies for her protection, including her physiotherapy.

For us as family, as for many, it has been a surreal and frightening experience and, on many occasions, my stomach has turned arabesques listening to the horrific figures and stories portrayed by the media and government alike.

Rachel's carers have still been in attendance 24 hours day and we have had to face new battles around securing PPE for them and insisting that they take every precaution to ensure she is not exposed to the virus.

The rest of the family have kept our distance from her as much as possible, and, so far, we have succeeded in protecting her. She has been as bright and bubbly, and as resilient as ever, despite it all. I have always tried to emphasise to all of Rachel's carers the importance of making her day as full of fun as possible, and this is now more important than ever as her social interactions with others are reduced.

Covid-19 has been a big challenge for us. As well as protecting Rachel, we have had my mother to consider, as she is now 85 and very vulnerable. My biggest fear though, was that if Rachel caught the virus and had to be admitted to hospital, I would not be able to go with her. I couldn't bear the thought of her being ill and alone, and possibly dying, on a Covid ward. Unable to communicate without me, she would be so distressed and confused.

We made the decision that if this did happen, we would not allow her to be admitted and I would nurse her at home, whatever the circumstances. Of course, the thought of having to go through this on our own, with no family allowed to be with us, fills me with dread, but for Rachel's sake, I feel we would have no choice in the matter.

Overall, though, pandemics aside, life is good. We

have settled into an easy routine that works well for us all. She has a team of six carers, who work in shifts. Most of them have worked with us for many years and fully understand her needs and her personality. She requires "waking" carers at night due to her double incontinence, the fact that she has fluids delivered overnight via a pump through her BGT, and to keep a watchful eye out for any seizures.

The BGT has been a godsend. She still enjoys three good meals a day by mouth, but because her medication is delivered through it, her epilepsy remains well-controlled and she is always well-hydrated, even in the extreme temperatures we have experienced in the summer of 2020.

She has a programme of home-based therapies, including aromatherapy, music therapy, massage, Reiki and physiotherapy. We take her out for walks in her wheelchair and have a specially adapted vehicle, which enables us to take her to concerts and to the theatre. She still loves music and, although she has a very eclectic taste ranging from classical to calypso, her favourite band by far is still ABBA. I think if Rachel was able to talk, she would tell you that her life is good, and that most of the time she is very happy.

She loves company and absolutely adores parties and family get-togethers. We celebrate every birthday with a big party, and we always make Christmas a big deal for her. She loves her carers and they adore her. She enjoys frequent visits from Giles, and her friends and family. My mother lives with us now in a "Granny Annex" extension, and we get regular visits from the whole extended family. Sadly, almost all her peers from school have long since passed away, but David is still her best friend (some might say boyfriend) and he visits as often as possible. Every day, the house is filled with the sound of her giggling and laughing. Nowadays, I work from home as a writer, and as I sit in my office working, the sounds of her laughter echoes across the hallway, which always brings a smile to my face. It's the most important sound in the world for me to hear.

All the other children have grown up and moved on. Steve spends most of his spare time looking after the garden. His boys live in London and Nottingham. Katie is married and lives in Belgium. A couple of years ago, she presented us with a beautiful little granddaughter. Brooke and her boyfriend now live and work in Australia. Rachel is always overjoyed to see all of her siblings, and they her, whenever they return home for visits.

Steve and I have a busy social life. I still feel the need to get out of the house regularly to help me manage my PTSD. We have a couple of adorable Labradors, Revel and Haribo, who keep us active. Our home will always be a busy place, full of carers and therapists, and comings and goings, and it is difficult to "switch off " and relax in this type of environment. So, getting to take time out from it is vitally important for our own mental health. This has been particularly hard during "lockdown", but I am incredibly lucky that I enjoy writing so much, as this has proved to be both a pleasure and a distraction.

Over the last few years, we have made it a policy to take a holiday whenever possible. I see it as our version of "respite". Rachel is happiest at home and I know she would not enjoy being sent away for respite care, so instead, we are the ones who go away. I know she is always well-looked after, and the carers never hesitate to get in touch if there are any problems. We often use these trips to catch up with Katie and Brooke and my loyal and loving friend, Louise. We are very fortunate to be in the luxurious position of being able to do this whenever we can, and I am constantly reminding myself of this.

Don't get me wrong, we still have our challenges and always will. I run Rachel's affairs like a business, which is time-consuming and can be stressful. We do have issues with carers leaving, or letting us down, from time to time. We face constant and ongoing battles with the attitudes and behaviours of others towards people with disabilities. While I can usually find it in me to make excuses for people who do not know any better, it is especially hard to deal with it in people who should. And, when the very services that have been set up to support families like ours let us down, as they do on frequent occasions, I simply despair.

For example, when we moved to our new house, despite trying to avoid this, we did have an issue with Rachel's care package. It's a very long story but it involved a misunderstanding around our new postcode, the local authority accusing us of fraud and refusing to pay for her care. It even resulted in them placing a debt of many thousands of pounds against her name and the bailiffs coming round. Suffice to say, it took several years of bitter wrangling between us and the two different local authorities, which ended with Steve and I holding a "sit-in" in their offices, before it was finally resolved. It turned out in the end that Rachel had over-paid for her care to the sum of £80,000!

On another occasion, I dabbled with the idea of sending Rachel to daycare to enhance her social life. This ended in disaster when we found out that she was being excluded from many of the group activities because of a fear that her wheelchair could act as a missile were the transport vehicle to be involved in a road traffic accident. I could have understood this to a degree, if the transport vehicle hadn't been the same one that took her to and from the centre every day!

I could go on and list many more examples, but I have tried to simplify and summarise some of the main issues and disputes we have faced over the years. Sadly, my experiences with the NHS, social services and local authorities have not been good, and I know I am not alone. I have lost count of the number of people I have met who have faced similar situations. These services are hugely important in many people's lives and whilst I feel the NHS do a lot of good work and have done particularly well during the pandemic, I truly believe it is time for the system to have a major overhaul of the way it is managed. Mistakes are still being made and babies are still being damaged, or even worse, dying, in overcrowded and underfunded maternity wards. My experiences of dealing with social services and local authorities has led me to believe that they are so engrained in the culture of protecting their budgets, that they lose sight of the very people they are being paid to assist.

Naively, I assumed that all these services would go out of their way to help and support people like Rachel and families like ours. Whilst I believe that clinicians, carers and social workers do, largely, have the best interests of their patients and clients at heart, they too are often at the mercy of unscrupulous and money-driven bureaucrats, who fail to see the impact of their actions on the people involved. Every day they are battling staff shortages, budget cuts and a demand for care that far outstrips their capacity, which inevitably has an impact on the quality of care that they are able to provide. All too often, I have heard the words, "We have got to protect our budget!", and "We don't have the resources!". Maybe it's time for things to change, but it has to start at the very top.

Thankfully, Rachel does not cry very often, and she never cries for no reason, but for me, when she does, it is the most heart-wrenching experience. I always feel so helpless, as she is unable to indicate why she is distressed. As her mother, this is probably the most difficult thing, other than the seizures, to have to deal with.

The worst moments for us during the Covid-19 crisis have been when Rachel has had severe muscle spasms due to her not having her usual physiotherapy regime. A few months into "lockdown" she started having screaming episodes. She was obviously in pain but, at first, we didn't know where the pain was and how to deal with it. Sometimes she screams when she has an aura before a seizure, and we initially tried her seizure rescue medication which acts as a sedative. It helped a little but when it wore off, she just started screaming again.

It must be so distressing for Rachel not to be able to tell us the reason why she is screaming. I can't even begin to imagine how she must feel, when no-one understands her. When there is nothing obvious, it is purely a process of elimination,

On a few occasions, she has screamed on and off

for several hours. Rachel has an extremely high pain threshold, so I knew. when that happened, she must be in terrible pain. But I was so fearful of taking her to hospital. I couldn't decide what to do for the best. Once again, I felt so helpless. I broke my social distancing ruling to comfort and reassure her. We had several telephone consultations with our GP. We tried paracetamol and ibuprofen but nothing seemed to help. We were completely baffled as to the cause.

These episodes came and went over a couple of weeks, until one day, she screamed continuously for 15 minutes. I had no choice but to call an ambulance. My worst fear was becoming a reality.

The paramedics were wonderful. They could see right away that she was in severe pain. They gave her a dose of morphine, and within a few minutes she had calmed down. But they insisted that she should be checked over in hospital as we didn't really know what was causing the pain.

I was terrified, but because of her situation, they allowed me to go with her. They reassured me that we would be going to a city centre hospital, where they had strict and clearly separated Covid-19 "cold" and "hot" areas, and she would always be stringently protected. I struggled through the entire journey, shaking uncontrollably, whilst trying to reassure Rachel that everything was going to be okay.

Of course, they were right. We spent a few hours in A&E while they conducted multiple investigations. Everyone was in full PPE and adhered to strict virus transmission prevention protocols. I had to wear a face mask the entire time, and they even tried to get Rachel to wear one. She wasn't having any of it! One nurse tried several times to put one on her face but she twisted her head from side to side, and made such a fuss that the nurse gave up, saying, "I'll take that as a no then!".

"Hell, yeah!" I said. "If Rachel decides it's not happening, as disabled as she is, she'll find a way to let you know."

All the tests came back clear, and it was agreed that the most likely cause of her pain was muscle spasms. She was prescribed a muscle relaxant and morphine for when it became really bad. After we got home, we decided to restart her physiotherapy sessions, and so far, she hasn't had a single recurrence, much to our delight.

It has certainly been the strangest summer of our lives. We have no idea what the future will hold for Rachel as we enter a second wave of the virus. I worry that, if she remains healthy, I may outlive her one day and what might happen to her then? But the alternative of her going before me does not bear thinking about. For the moment, I am content that she is still here and is still enjoying every moment of her life. To me, she is the important one.

One of the big things I have learned from Rachel, is to live in the moment. But I have learned other things from her, too. My biggest sorrow is that she is unable to communicate in a conventional manner. I would love to be able to know her thoughts, her feelings. Whilst I can guess at obvious things like pleasure or displeasure, I will never know exactly what goes on inside her mind.

I have been inspired by her strength, determination, and cheerfulness, despite everything she has faced and may face in the future. She has taught me not to "sweat the small stuff". Rachel's life puts all the trivial everyday problems that we all complain about from time to time into stark perspective. On the night she was born, and we were told that she might not survive until morning, all the material things that had seemed so important to me before, suddenly became meaningless.

She may not look or act like everyone else, but I don't need her to. I love Rachel just for the very special soul that she is.

She's taught me patience and the ability to have empathy for others who are suffering. When I'm having a bad day, I just have to spend a few minutes with her, and her infectious smiles and laughter, and I feel renewed. How can I possibly feel down or complain when I have so much, and she is happy and content with so little. I never take anything for granted, and I live a fuller life than I might have done if she hadn't been in it.

I would be lying if I didn't say that, at times, I've felt overwhelmed with the responsibility of being Rachel's mother. I have carried much guilt that she is unable to fulfill her life in ways I wish she'd been able to ... in the same way that her sisters have. But she has taught me what true, unconditional love is: the purest form of love there is. She has never once uttered a hurtful word or behaved in a hurtful way towards me. She is my angel, and although there have been tears and heartbreak over the years, I wouldn't change her for anything.

She is my Rachel, unique and very, very special. There is no one like her in the world.

Footnote

It is not just me who has benefitted from having Rachel in my life; the whole family has, too. These are their words.

Steve (My husband and Rachel's stepfather)

I think it's impossible to tell Rachel's story without it being Shelley's story as well. The two of them are forever integrally entwined, with an unbreakable bond cemented in love.

Shelley has selflessly devoted herself to Rachel's care and wellbeing for some 33 years. She continues to give Rachel all the love and attention, she requires. On top of that, she has fought tirelessly on Rachel's behalf.

I know all mothers love their children, however they grow and their needs change in time. Therefore our roles as parents also change accordingly, as they develop into adults. Rachel's mental progress has never developed much past the stage of a six-month-old, however she has grown into an adult with major and complex needs.

Rachel is totally dependent on the care she receives from us as a family and her team of carers. Shelley's love for Rachel has never wavered, with all the challenges, trial and tribulations, which go hand in hand for caring for someone with cerebral palsy. This is a big part of what made me fall in love with her, in the first place, her loving caring nature.

Rachel too has showed me so much about life. She has taught me so much without ever saying a word. Her smile and laughter are infectious, also that mischievous look in her eyes. She won me over immediately. She continues to amaze me with her love of life. She has also taught me a liking for Abba's music! The enjoyment Rachel has for all music, but especially Abba is awe-inspiring.

Rachel is an amazing young lady and that's what I love about her.

Nanny (My mum and Rachel's grandmother)

I admire my daughter for writing this book about my very special granddaughter. It must have been very upsetting at times. I know as a fact that she has had to fight so hard at different times in her daughter's life for various things she needed. I am amazed at the determination she has to change the way society views her daughter's disability.

Although my granddaughter cannot do anything for herself, to me she is perfect, and I love and treat her the same as my other grandchildren and my great grandchild. I tell her that she is my No. 1 and she loves that and always has a giggle. I read books to her, which you can tell she is understanding. When I am ironing, she loves it when I sing to her. I tell her stories of the past, which amuses her. Christmas and birthdays are an exciting time for her when she gets lots of presents and watches the Christmas Tree being decorated.

You can see from every page of this book, that from the start it has been a hard journey for the family. One learns to understand a grandchild with cerebral palsy and what their lives are like. You see what is like for the families to take care of them. You see how people who don't understand can be cruel to them (perhaps not deliberately). Golly, by reading this book I hope you don't realise you are one of these people. People like Rachel deserve to be treated exactly as you and me. I know that my granddaughter has lots of love to give, happiness and a very contagious smile. I know I am blessed to have her in my life.

James (Steve's son and Rachel's stepbrother)

Rachel has taught me always to smile. Her strength and resilience mean she is very special to us all and she has enriched my life by always making me laugh and smile whenever I see her. She is such a wonderful person and I'm proud to call her my sister.

About The Authors

J.M McKenzie

J.M. McKenzie describes herself as an aspiring writer. She has had a long career in healthcare and science but always dreamed of writing full-time. She has published in scientific journals but, yearns to write fiction. She is currently working on the second draft of her first novel, *Wait for Me*, a love story set in a zombie apocalypse. She has recently retired from full-time employment to focus on developing her writing and has self-published a short story, *Puschkinia,* on Kindle Direct Publishing.

S.J. Gibbs

S.J.'s love of reading and writing started at a very young age and, as a teenager, she would often be found with her nose in a book or reading under the bedclothes with a torch after her father had turned out her bedroom light.

After leaving school, in her spare time, she wrote short stories for her own pleasure, but reading was still her passion.

In 1987, her first daughter, Rachel, was born and diagnosed with cerebral palsy. This prompted her to start writhing this novel about the struggles of bringing up a daughter with a profound disability. This became a joint project with J.M. McKenzie, as she was struggling with the emotions of trying to write about her daughter's life.

At the beginning of 2015, S.J.'s writing began in earnest after joining DH Writer Group.

She successfully completed the Writers Bureau Creative Writing Course, which she thoroughly enjoyed.

She is also involved in a collaborative novel started by the writers group.

She has completed the first draft of her novel "The Cutting Edge", which is aimed at the young adult market, and editing is her current main focus.

A short story 'Fighting A Battle with Himself' has been written, edited and published, and is available on Amazon.

She has also co-written a book, 'The Secrets to healing with Clear Quartz Crystal,' which has also been published and is available on Amazon.

Printed in Great Britain
by Amazon